ADVANCE PRAISE FOR
HOW TO WRITE A SONG THAT MATTERS

"Long ago on a hot, late summer night I was driving alone on a beach road, the shadows of my headlights slicing the humid air amidst a million bugs in V formation, while the local radio station played a song called 'Are You Out There' by Dar Williams. It was one of those startling, magical instances where the song I was hearing made me feel more alive and less alone, the way the best songs do. And I felt connected to something invisible and mysterious—that whoever wrote that song *knew* what I was feeling. When Dar and I became friends years later, that was the first thing I wanted to share and to thank her for—for writing a song that mattered to me. In this beautiful and wise book, she explores how a song can matter in many different ways, to different people, for different reasons. The wisdom and the lessons she shares will illuminate not only the world of songwriters but anyone who seeks the sustenance of a creative life and practice."

—Mary Chapin Carpenter, Grammy award-
winning singer-songwriter

"There are songs that have changed my life, described my life, upped my life, saved my life. I wear those songs like charms on a bracelet. Several of those charms were written by the glorious Dar Williams. As Dar says in this gem of a book, *How to Write A Song that Matters*, 'When I hear a song that I love, something catches and holds me the way gravity holds us to the ground.' And then she takes us deep into the process of creating a song (or a poem, a book, a pot of soup) so that we too can offer others the charms they need to ground their lives with meaning...a healing charm, a power charm, a beauty charm. Thank you, Dar. I'll keep coming back to this book for inspiration and direction."

—Elizabeth Lesser, cofounder, Omega Institute,
and author of bestselling books including *Broken Open* and *Cassandra Speaks*

HOW TO WRITE A SONG THAT MATTERS

Also by Dar Williams

What I Found in a Thousand Towns: A Traveling Musician's Guide to Rebuilding America's Communities—One Coffee Shop, Dog Run, and Open-Mike Night at a Time

Amalee

Lights, Camera, Amalee

HOW TO WRITE A SONG THAT MATTERS

DAR WILLIAMS

hachette
BOOKS

New York

Hachette Books
Hachette Book Group
1290 Avenue of the Americas
New York, NY 10104
HachetteBooks.com
Twitter.com/HachetteBooks
Instagram.com/HachetteBooks

First Edition: September 2022

Published by Hachette Books, an imprint of Perseus Books, LLC, a subsidiary of Hachette Book Group, Inc. The Hachette Books name and logo is a trademark of the Hachette Book Group.

The Hachette Speakers Bureau provides a wide range of authors for speaking events. To find out more, go to www.hachettespeakersbureau.com or call (866) 376-6591.

The publisher is not responsible for websites (or their content) that are not owned by the publisher.

Interior illustrations by Katryna Nields.

Lyric credits:
  "Cold Missouri Waters" by James Keelaghan © Tranquila Music, 1995
  "On the Eve of the Inaugural" by Peter Mulvey © September Dawn Music (ASCAP), 2021
  "Can't Fall Down" by Jim Infantino © Funny/Not Funny Music (ASCAP), 1995
  "The Driver's Song" written by Bill Morrissey © DryFly Music, 1989
  "Chasing Daylight" by Lisa Forkish © Lisa Forkish Music, 2014

Print book interior design by Amy Quinn.

Library of Congress Cataloging-in-Publication Data has been applied for.

ISBNs: 9780306923296 (trade paperback); 9780306923289 (ebook)

Printed in the United States of America

LSC-C

Printing 1, 2022

For Raquel Vidal, Rick Gedney, and Michele Gedney, my pillars.
And Toby Shimin.

CONTENTS

INTRODUCTION(S) 1

INSPIRATION 9

NARRATIVE 47

WORDS 113

MUSIC (IN OTHER WORDS...) 151

CROSSROADS AND ENDINGS 185

BRINGING OUR SONGS INTO THE WORLD 217

THE SONGWRITER (YOU AND ME) 251

ACKNOWLEDGMENTS 275

INTRODUCTION(S)

INTRODUCTION

When I was a boy . . .

The phrase popped in my head with a little bit of melody. I knew it was going to be a song. I understood what I had to do. I had to clear as much time and space around this moment as I could, getting a sense of why the phrase had struck me. I had to approach this short line of music and lyrics with confidence, but also with care, listening to the song as I created it. What clues was I getting from the words, the rhythm, and the feel of this phrase? Where was it taking me?

I gently inquired if "When I was *like* a boy" might be more accurate. Isn't gender just a construct? Is there such a thing as *being* a boy these days? The new phrase, swirling in my head, responded gently. "It's not when I was *like* a boy. It's when I *was* a boy."

My friend Jaimé Morton had taught me a new guitar tuning called D–A–D–G–A–D. I played the phrase on the guitar and started messing with the chords around it. I didn't know their names. Jaimé had just taught me how to go up and down the fretboard with the same chord shape, so that's what I did.

Over the next few weeks, with and without my guitar, I started pulling in information, writing couplets, then verses, about that time when I was "a boy." I'd just heard Judy Kaye's version of a Leonard Bernstein song, "Dream with Me," sung by Wendy to Peter in a telling of the children's story *Peter Pan*. "Dream with Me" suggested that Wendy was a little in love with Peter Pan, but she also loved being one of his fellow adventurers. I was that Wendy, at twelve, a little in love with the boys who tackled me in football.

I compiled other memories of being in the woods, being on a bike, and being with the other boys. I wrote two verses over two months. Each verse included some aspect of my boyhood freedom, coupled with my limitations as a grown woman.

The feminists are going to kill me, I kept thinking. I was living in Northampton, the lesbian mecca of Massachusetts, its own Neverland for girls who didn't need boys at all. Why would a woman call her childhood her boyhood? But the phrase was insistent. I kept on listening and letting the song unfurl.

I'd come to the third verse. How would I end this song? What was the truth? What *really* happened?

I realized that even though I had lost some of my childhood freedom as a woman, I knew I was part of a movement that was bringing more freedoms and rights to more women. Should I end the song with something about the women's movement or some other feminist theme?

I also started thinking about how the joyful memory of being "a boy" was something I could talk about with some of my friends. Feminist ideology aside, I had compatriots whom I knew would understand this gender experience. At that moment, my mind brought me to the subject of the final verse.

I was going to turn the focus on . . . *men.*

Scores of male friends had confided in me over the years. Their common refrain was "I'm not like other men, and I can't talk with other men about it."

And there it was. I knew how I was going to end the song. The narrator would be hanging out with a man. He would talk about what he lost when he became an adult, and he would begin by saying, *When I was a girl.*

My musician roommate, a radical feminist, heard the song and said, right off the bat, "Whoa. Why did you end with a dude?"

But this was the song I felt compelled to write, so this is the song I wrote.

A few days later, I was a last-minute addition in a round-robin concert, and we playing songs based on phrases taken out of a hat. One scrap of paper said, "Come up to my treehouse." We murmured among ourselves, and my friend said, "Why don't you play that new one?"

The applause at the end of my new song, "When I Was a Boy," was very strange. There were no hoots or whistles, but the clapping was notably sustained. After the show, a young woman approached me. I girded myself. Big feminist.

"I just wanted you to know," she said, "I really appreciated that song, and . . . yeah, I did." She walked away.

No one was rushing for her pitchfork. One by one, I heard, "Cool song." And "I liked the new one." But the biggest surprise came when I was standing off to the side in the shadows. A tall man stood next to me and said, "I was a girl."

Then he smiled, as if to say, "I know! Me!"

"When I Was a Boy" launched my career. I didn't know, in the mid-1990s, that conversations about feminism and sexual orientation were becoming deeper inquiries about what it was to be male and female. I didn't know that feminists would understand what it meant to feel that "boy" feeling in my blood as a child. I didn't know how many men would talk with me and write me letters about their gender identities. I just knew the song was true for me and that it mattered to me to write it. This was the song that strengthened my resolve to pursue all my songs on their own terms, with all the whimsy and curiosity I had learned to apply to the process, but also with some personal courage. This song and its success reinforced a sense that listening for cues and clues of what *really happened* for my narrator, not just what I thought *should happen,* was important. Writing about what mattered to me had a purpose.

In 2013 I started leading songwriting retreats and discovered that I was finding names for the steps we were taking to write a song from start to finish. I noticed that we weren't just discovering the stages of a song; we were defining the steps that a *songwriter* takes in transforming a first inspiration into a finished song. This book distills a process that's shared by me, my colleagues, and hundreds of songwriters from the ever-evolving exploration of how we write our songs.

People have very different ways of beginning songs and staying the course in writing them. That's why we say we lead, not teach, retreats and workshops. My effort has been to show how we were able to write songs that mattered to us. And, now, nothing would make me happier than to help you, songwriters I have met or have yet to meet, on the path to writing a song that matters to you, and . . . who knows?

YOU DON'T HAVE TO PLAY AN INSTRUMENT

A common concern that people have is how they can write songs if they don't play an instrument outside the instrument of the voice. Many of the musical references in this book are to chord structures, and a few of them are described (different tunings and hand shapes) in terms of how I have come to them as a guitar player.

Here are some ideas for working with music when we don't play an instrument:

1. We can bring our thoughts and questions to someone who plays an instrument and see if we can collaborate.
2. If we're hearing certain chords or cadences under a melody we're writing, we can go to a piano, pick out chords by ear, and record the chords for reference.
3. There is something called a "baritone ukulele" that has four strings that are the same notes as the high strings of a guitar. So, it's a guitar with four strings instead of six. Ukes are lighter and easier to play than guitars, generally. We can do a lot with just a few two- or three-fingered chords (which translate to playing a six-stringed guitar later on if the desire is there).

4. Know that many songs can be written with only seven or eight chords, tops (or even three). A little instrument learning goes a long way to help unlock many forms of musical communication!

However you join music with your lyrics, please, please, just jump over things in this book that don't relate to your songwriting or that are intimidating in general.

INSPIRATION

THINKING POETICALLY

Here are some words: "door," "key," "road," "river." Perhaps these words will be part of what we're doing today. We're going out the door, we've got our keys, and we're going down a road next to a river. These are the words of things that are getting us from here to there.

Now, read the same words, but think of them poetically: "door," "key," "road," "river."

Did you feel a difference in your thinking? I feel a difference between thinking about words objectively, as connectors from point A to point B, and subjectively, as the poetic vehicles of how I experience the world. These words take on different meanings when they are the subject of our thinking, not the object.

The term "nuclear family" means one's immediate family. Poetically, "nuclear family" can mean many other things.

Some people never turn off their poetic thinking. They see children running out of the school door at recess and think of water bursting out of a fire hose. A teapot becomes a metaphor for the entire British Empire.

Some people will consciously tune in to their poetic minds and reside in that space of poetic associations. I write songs for a living, so that's what I do.

Others feel like, once upon a time, they put their poetic thinking aside, and now they've lost it forever. That is a red-herring thought. There are many reasons we step away from a poetic perspective, but it's never "too late" to have one. Poetic thinking never ends, not with age, parenthood, grief, busy jobs, or the fervor of a political moment.

We all have the power to look at a phrase, a word, or a moment poetically, whether we are at a songwriting retreat, at a stoplight, or in the middle of a work meeting. Ideally, when we realize that we want to write a song, or an inspiring idea comes from out of the blue, we can set a little time aside to go with that surge of excitement that comes with its creative origins.

FOR EXAMPLE...

If you'd like to start right now, here we go. Look at any of the following words *poetically* and see what happens:

The playing field.
The fire escape.
The waiting room.

THAT FIRST INSPIRATION

I call it "The Window Opens."

Children's author Natasha Wing calls it "Getting the Tinglies."

Novelist Stephanie Kallos calls it "Open for Business."

There is a sensation we get when we know that something we've heard, or the thought we've just thought, has the makings of a work of art.

We just have that feeling: this full moon, this stone in my hand, or this strange headline has just presented itself in a certain way. I'm open for business; I get the tinglies; the window opens.

In 1994 my housemate, Sarah Davis, said, "I think you're going to want to write a song about this news story. There was an ice storm in Philadelphia, and the deejays asked people to turn off their electricity so they could power the hospitals. And everyone did."

That was interesting. I nodded my head. It was a good story about neighborliness. It was great fodder for someone's song, maybe not mine. Then Sarah added a detail.

"They said you could watch the lights going out in entire buildings. Even the businesses."

This wasn't just about neighbors. It was about civilization. A window opened. I wrote a long song called "Mortal City."

Natasha Wing heard that once upon a time there had been a plan to tear down Grand Central Station, but former first lady Jackie Onassis stepped in and saved it. That's when she said she got "what I call the tinglies." She wrote a best-selling children's book about Jackie O's campaign.

The best way to court inspiration is to simply pause and recognize when it has come to us. That moment of inspiration can be subtle, like a little shift, or a tingle.

COURTING INSPIRATION

And if inspiration doesn't come to us, the eternal question is: How do we get *there* when we're standing *here*, in a world of jamming copy machines, piles of dishes, and traffic-snarled work commutes?

When we deliberately set our course for "poetic thinking," looking at something from a different angle or letting our minds make their own associations, we might find ourselves at some emotional portal of fascination, a cross-section of feelings and curiosity. So, the decision to see the world poetically *renversé* (French for "overturned") could be a first step.

Another step is to *value* the time we spend looking at things differently and to give the search for inspiration a little effort if things don't go *renversé* at first glance. If I'm in a traffic jam in Waterbury, Connecticut, for instance, I'll look around and see if something opens a window.

The bumper sticker on the car in front of me doesn't inspire poetic possibilities. It just makes me mad. There's a baby in a car seat in the next lane. I think a baby could inspire something . . . but no. Nothing.

And then I look ahead and see that the highway divides the entire city in two. And a phrase comes into my mind, "The road between us." Something feels different. Something feels . . . poetic. What is the road between us? I think of a busy, modern thoroughfare that separates two people. Did someone jump into a car and take that road, while another cursed the road that presented such a convenient exit? I pick out pieces of an image and see what each of them signifies. Who is "us"? A couple? A family? What is "the road"? Is it a road of temptation, success, or escape? I ask questions and ponder the answers. When a window has opened, I look through it.

I discovered a formalized way to court inspiration, or enter into a place where I tended to think poetically, when I followed Julia Cameron's exercise in *The Artist's Way* (a book and a practice). I was tasked to create my ideal "artist date," a weekly time that's set aside for things I loved to do. I found out that walking along rivers, going to museums, and sneaking out to matinees of blockbuster movies were equally effective for opening the window.

I PLAY TO WORK,
I WORK TO PLAY

The motto I use in my profession is that "I play to work, and I work to play." What my songwriting friends and I have in common, as we court inspiration, is that we invite creative disruption into our minds and lives. We disorient ourselves in service of discovering new patterns, ordering systems, and poetic priorities that can help us in this artistic construction called a song. In other words, we work to find ways to play.

I used to think that by going to museums, the power of the artwork, like a tea bag in water, would infuse itself naturally into my psyche and inspire my songs. Now I know there is a mental middle step between my inspiration totems and the writing of a song. What a museum trip really did was jog my mind out of its list-making, breadwinning activities. Looking at other people's art took enough gravity out of everyday life to rearrange my linear, objective reality.

If I see a spider in my house, I find a way to get it out of my house. That's my activity. Maybe, as I convey the spider out the door on an old guitar string, I'll think of the spiderweb as a home within my home. I'll imagine a little spiderweb replica of my house. I'll allow my poetic thinking to disrupt the brain circuit of doing household jobs.

But if, in the course of keeping a house clean, I'm not entertaining metaphors and poetic perspectives, I can leave the house, go to the museum, and see Louise Bourgeois's room-size *Spider*. A spider will go from the object of my daily activities to the subject of my thinking about webs, homes, symmetry, secrets, fear, shame, and who knows what else. Museums are playgrounds for my mind.

If I don't have the time or opportunity to visit a museum, I'll try little things to alter my perspective. I'll strum a chord a little differently or stare at kitchen utensils. I always keep an available blank writing surface nearby, because I never know which of these little thought aberrations will be part of a song.

Jim Infantino wrote a whole song about a breakup from the perspective of lying on his kitchen floor.

> *Up there's the bottom of the shelf*
> *can't fall down from here*
> *I don't understand myself*
> *It's like when I was three*
> *can't fall down from here*
> *the underside of things I see . . .*

Sometimes song ideas come when a car passes and I mishear a melody blaring out the window. Or my ear creates a melody over the chord made by a steam pipe, refrigerator hum, and barking dog. We can listen for chords and cadences in the air.

I wake up with melodies and words left over from dreams. I have at least three songs that started with a single line from a dream. I've learned to entertain these floating melodies, bypassing my own first objections that "Obviously *this* can't be anything I would use."

I've been impressed by the range of what my friends do to jolt themselves into poetic thinking to write their songs.

Singer-songwriter Cliff Eberhardt had a small machine with different synth rhythms that he would play along with (and I know there are many rhythm apps now).

I overheard Ellis Paul talk about strumming the guitar while watching television with no sound.

Jules Shear used to wake himself up at three in the morning to write in a semidream state.

One retreater impressed me with his fail-safe method of coming up with a song title and writing a song from it.

Lucy Kaplansky listens to a lot of other people's music and then pulls out chords and cadences to play with.

All of these playful practices, catching ourselves at the periphery of sleep, going into a trance state, or entering an environment that excites memories and imagination, are methods for disorienting ourselves into the manna of poetic associations that become our songs.

FIRST CLUES

The tiniest phrase of words or music that comes into our heads, and whatever rhythms, chordal ambiance, or lyrics that accompany it, can yield clues to what the rest of the song might be.

I usually sing that first bit of a song to myself for a while (sometimes for days), just to make sure it's really planted in my head, and then I listen for the clues.

What is the rhythm? Is it a waltz, a march, a loose and rambling road song?

What is the register of the language? Is it the language of commerce, celebration, sadness, intimacy?

How does it feel? Do I hear cadences of dreamlike major sevenths, austere minor chords, splashy major chords?

Whatever comes to us with that first inspiration may seem really small and faint. There's a reason it's called a spark.

But no matter how unusual, sappy, silly, jazzy, vague, or disco those first sounds are, I always spend some time fanning that spark, looking for clues in case it is indeed the start of something. I never stamp out that little bit of light and heat.

I walked around with the first spark of the song, "After All," for a long time, and it was, simply, a four-note melody with the words "And it felt like . . ."

It felt like what? What was "it"? The answer came very slowly. I gave it the time and followed the clues. *It's subtle; it's searching; it's conversational; it's straightforward 4/4 time . . .*

Musically, we can start placing elements of a melody fragment in other parts of the song. There might be a triplet, a wide interval, or a rapid fire of four notes that we hear as a verse. We can experiment with that form and hear if it fits in another part of the verse or in a chorus. We can take that little piece to understand the inner mechanics of a song that's starting to emerge. It can also have a genre feel to it, like bossa nova or bluegrass.

I don't always know the musical terms for what I'm hearing. I might say it has a little "shake-me-up" (a triplet) or a big space between notes (a wide interval), or that it sounds like the music we've heard in old horror movies (alternating major and minor of a chord). Whatever way we hear a motif, we can locate that particular sound in other parts of the song, repeating or modifying the melodies and rhythms so that they're consistent, but not the same.

If it feels too soon to identify these little musical signatures, there is always methodical trial and error. As Tom Prasada-Rao says, "When in doubt, repeat." If I've got three notes, I'll try repeating them, then I'll try repeating them with one different note, and then I go up, and then down, until I find something I like.

Since I play an instrument, I'll find the key of that musical phrase and play it on my guitar to get a better sense of the chords and the ambiance that might surround it.

I do all that experimenting and picking around. Sometimes, in fact, an even more interesting motif appears a line or two later. But with that first fragment of whatever it is, I find it helpful to track down all the clues I can and see what they might reveal in the larger identity of a song.

AMBIANCE

It took me a while to arrive at the word "ambiance" for the musical atmosphere of chords, and sequences of chords, that hangs in the air around a melody.

"Ambiance" comes from Latin words that mean "go around." I call the sounds of chords, and the movement between them, the ambiance of our first inspiration.

Have you ever captured a piece of melody in a quick recording, only to replay it later and think, "What was special about that?" When we hear that single line of notes later on, we might not be hearing the bed of chords that originally lay underneath the melody in our heads when it grabbed us. It's the musical ambiance that will determine the minor-chord feel of chilly rain or the major-seventh feel of a spring morning. I often record a harmony line or the three notes of the chord that I hear under the melody just to make sure I'm in the musical world that I imagined. I am convinced that when I'm captivated by a melody, the beautifully faceted, opalescent ambiance surrounding it is what actually holds my attention.

For the guitar players out there, here's an example: find the Lyle Lovett song "Closing Time" and pluck at the chords of just the first line: *The night, she is a true companion.* Start the lyric with a G chord, and end it with an Em (minor). If you're feeling fancy, you can "walk it down," hitting a G chord with an F# (sharp) in the low E string on the way down to the Em.

G [G(F#)] Em

The night, she is a true companion . . .

Now try the same thing, but when you make the Em chord, move the finger on the D string up two frets. Even if you are a beginning guitarist, you can do this! Now the Em becomes an Em "add 9."

G [G(F#)] Em "add 9"

The night, she is a true companion . . .

The ambiance experiences of that first line, just by moving one finger two frets, are very different. Poetically, they are worlds apart.

We will talk about how to make chords, how to move between them, and how we can appreciate their narrative role. You can go there now by looking at the chapters "Chord Houses" and "Wonderful, Wonderful Chords."

But at this beginning phase, as we move from capturing inspiration into creating a song, one great way to start, with or without chords, is to find a way to catch the ambiance that surrounds the first inspiration.

MAKE IT PRETTY

It's hard to grab hold of the things we write if they don't grab hold of us first. The feeling of "I like this. This sounds good to me" can be an essential motivator for continuing our songs. I always know I'm on my way when a song sounds pretty to me.

Getting to the point of "I like this" is usually a matter of playing out a lot of options for myself. I'm guided by the emerging clues of the song, but I'm also listening for something that I simply like to hear. I had a sequence of two minor chords that recently popped into my head with the words "There's a light rain falling on the night train . . ." It had a loose and strummy feeling, with a playful interior rhyme. It was a little melancholy, but more emotionally reflective than depressed. Got it. With that information, I started my trial and error of chords and words just based on what I thought sounded good.

What is pleasing, alluring, or at least interesting to us is significant. I can't tell you the number of times I put a song aside, assuming it just didn't "work," only to realize that I just didn't like it. The secret was to pick the fledgling song back up and rework it until the lines were pleasant to my ear and interesting to my mind. Listening for what rings my inner bells is the best way to keep myself engaged and excited as I go along.

THE SOUNDS

Just as we follow our inspirations by creating something that is pretty to our ears, we can feel around for a lyric, or all of the lyrics, by filling our first melodic lines with nonword sounds we like, just to get a sense of what feels right. When I get my melodic ideas, they might come with an "aaah" or "oooh" sound that often corresponds to the word I'll use. Beth Nielsen Chapman says she often starts a song with just vowels, not consonants or words, as she feels her way along.

Some songwriters and poets have gone so far as to create sonic tapestries that just have interesting sounds, and they qualify as artistic compositions in their own right, as we know from learning Lewis Carroll's lines "'Twas brillig, and the slithy toves / Did gyre and gimble in the wabe" at school. The listener's ear can respond to an interesting sonic landscape even if the words don't make sense.

Most of us, however, want a song with more narrative than just vocal ambiance. The lyricism of certain sounds can still help us take a first stab at knowing what our songs will be. I had a vocal exercise with a drawn out "I," "oh," and "ah" sound. The exercise with those sounds became the melody of a chorus. I started singing the word "Iowa" and realized that I wanted to write a song called "Iowa." Sounds can show us what will appeal to the ear, and they can also be a narrative portal.

EXPLORING LOOSELY

Looking for clues of how the song will unfold, lyrically and musically, is always a loose process for me. I let my mind wander over words and images, taking them in as I walk, cook, clean out a junk drawer, or stare at a bookshelf while I'm sitting on the couch with my guitar. I often let my mind go into a very soft focus.

For example, I was taking some groceries out of my car, and I heard twelve notes of melody in one go. It comprised two six-note lines: "Laluhlalala LAH, Laluhlalala LAH." I let them play over and over in my head as I collected clues and started my loose exploration. It was in regular 4/4 time, but it had a bounce to it. It had . . . a jauntiness? Yes, jaunty. What's jaunty? An image came up of Maurice Chevalier, a French gentleman performer who often wore a boater hat and sang songs like "Thank Heaven for Little Girls."

I heard Maurice singing my lines. I imagined some slightly leering song where he would be comparing different women, like, "There's a tall and a *short,* / A brunette and a *blond.*" I wasn't going to write *that* song, but I kept the bounce in the melody, and I noted the breezy spirit as well. The boater hat.

I brought this little melody down to Nashville, and it became a song, "Slippery Slope," that I wrote with Jim Lauderdale about the staying power of marriage. The song kept its "there's a this and a that" quality in the chorus with lines like "You're my beacon of light, / You're my noblest fight," and "There's a twist and a turn, / There's a bridge you can burn."

I combined the feel of the melody with something that was interesting to me (and Jim, in this case).

Checking in with what is interesting to us is another way to figure out how to proceed.

WHAT'S UP WITH ME?

As I pick up my clues and listen for chords and cadences, if I'm still unclear about where my song is going, I ask myself, "What's up with me?" I ask myself what's on my mind and what's interesting to me, and I ask myself these questions in the gentlest, easiest way possible (again, exploring loosely), letting images and ideas rise to the surface.

There's always something *bugging* me, so of course that's what's up with me. There's always an injustice in the world, and that's always up with me, too. My poetic imagination, however, might be interested in other things beyond the hot-button topics, and it might be more interested in nuances than in direct observations.

I proceed gingerly, because it might not be clear to me at first why I really want to write a song about, say, a midwife in colonial Massachusetts, as I did in the song "Holly Tree."

It started when I saw a nest in the hollow of a tree. I heard a melody with the words "I saw a nest in a tree hollow-oh." The line sounded like the tagline of an Appalachian ballad like "Silver Dagger," a song with a pleasant melody and a story of menace and murder. So, I was hearing something that had an "olden-times" folk-song feel, with simple major and minor chords. There was an ambiance of mystery in the music. Those were my first clues and cadences. I let my mind wander to memories of other "nests in trees," like the robins who had built a nest every spring in a holly tree outside my parents' house. I always experienced the robins' return as a clear sign of spring and hope.

Then my mind wandered over to times in history when plants were all symbols for things like purity, love, and kindness. I thought, "The symbolism of a robin's nest built in thorny holly leaves could be that life can win, even within precarious circumstances." Then I checked in with what moved me, what in "olden times" had struck me recently. A journalist had visited my dressing room with the book *The Devil in the Shape of a Woman*, by Carol Karlsen, and he told me that calling women "witches" in colonial Salem, Massachusetts, was a way to get widows off their farms so that other people could profit from their real estate. A line popped into my head that ended with "farm widow-oh."

I'd also read that herbal medicine was banned in parts of the American colonies, probably because herbal remedies cut into the business and credibility of doctors. Hence, the song "Holly Tree" tells a story of a widowed midwife administering herbs to another widow who is in labor. Soon the arbiters of colonial justice arrive, and though we don't see what happens, suddenly there is no midwife, nor mother, nor baby, just a new farmer being welcomed by the pastor who calls this property, ironically, "promised land." I realized in retrospect that, creatively, this was my way of addressing the "profit over people disguised as good business" headlines of the day.

I let these beginnings of a song roll out for a while, and then I engage with them by sensing what stories might *move* me or *strike* me in some way, looking at both the song and my life for helpful information.

WRITING WHEN WE'RE *ALMOST* FULL CIRCLE, EMOTIONALLY

I try to avoid getting emotionally bogged down when I'm asking "what's up" with myself. I look at where there's some measure of emotional separation between me and a conflict I've experienced.

If you are someone who can describe lightning as it's striking, I think that's wonderful. I tend to write after the lightning has struck.

I like being able to walk around something instead of standing (or feeling paralyzed) in it or in front of it. I like the extra context I get when I can walk *almost* 360 degrees around my thought or memory. I say *almost* because when I can't see *all* the way around something, my curiosity propels me forward. My pursuit of understanding—trying to find that elusive full circle resolution—lets me (and my song) be enlightened and illuminated by the answers I find as I go.

I started writing the song "February" a year and a half after a breakup. The breakup still hurt, but my defensive, humiliated, fault-finding anger was gone. I didn't want to accuse. I wanted to find closure and meaning on the other side of the split. I'd say I was at the 270-degree mark in the circle. Between the 270 degrees worth of acquired wisdom about love and life and the 90 degrees of emotions that still shook me when I thought too long about the breakup, I was able to write,

> You know I think Christmas was a long red glare,
> Shot up like a warning.
> We gave presents without cards.
> And then the snow came.
> We were always out shoveling.
> Then we'd drop to sleep exhausted.
> And we'd wake up,
> And it's snowing.

It still ached to remember, but I could see the recurring themes of freezing and forgetting. Beyond the scramble to accuse and blame, I could see we all had a role in the story. Our anger, expressed and unexpressed, had a role. Our unintentional emotional distancing played a role. Winter was both a metaphor and a participant in our undoing. The song felt like it had more honesty and insight when there was a space between me and the emotions that had once been boiling inside me. But I'm glad that, somewhere, the emotions, and their intensity, were still at a simmer.

CHORD HOUSES

Chords live in harmonious houses. Technically, they live in keys, but I call them houses.

In the house of the G chord (G major, that is), we also have the C chord and D chord. They are the chords that "go with" a G chord when we're building most songs in Western Hemisphere cultures.

In these houses, every chord has its housemates. In the house of D, the housemates are G and A.

In the house of C, the housemates are F and G.

Here's a picture:

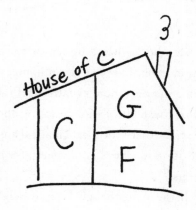

On a scale of notes, the names of these housemate chords are 2.5 (5 semitones) and 3.5 (7 semitones) whole notes away from the "1" (the original note or chord). So, when in doubt, we can count 2.5 and 3.5 whole notes away (but remember that E and F are only a half note away from each other, and so are B and C . . . I apologize for this confusion on behalf of the Western scale). This means that an F chord's housemates, for instance, are Bb (B flat major) and C.

Here's a picture:

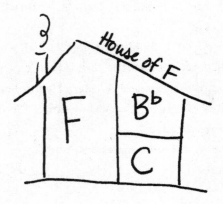

Every chord in each house has a bunch of variations that go with it, such as minor, seventh, major seventh, and minor seventh chords. There's even a major minor seventh. And there are sixths, too. Again, we get to these chords by counting the distance between notes on the scale. That's the mathematical approach to finding them, and there are also charts and wheels, for easy reference, that do the math for us.

Stepping away from the math, though, I like to call these variations on the chords "moods." Basically, we have three housemates with a range of moods, such as the sad (the minor), the in-between (the seventh and minor seventh), and the mellow (the major seventh).

In the house of G, we'll have the emotional reach of the G chord itself (Em, G7, Em7) and those of its housemates: C (Am, C7, Am7) and D (Bm, D7, Bm7).

There are all sorts of open, suspended, and amended versions of these chords, too, but let's just stick to a picture of the most used chords in this already-bustling house:

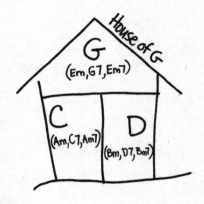

BORROWING A CHORD FROM THE NEIGHBOR'S HOUSE

So, let's say we're sussing out a melody, feeling out the moods, and listening for the right ambiance within our chord house, and we hit upon an emotion that's a little outside of this chord house. There's a particular piquancy, yearning, or even the cadences of a different musical genre that pop into our heads.

Here's something to help us discover new moods without just winging off into pure randomness (or brilliant jazz, whichever comes first): we can visit a neighboring house, often one that has a house-mate in common with our original house.

Here's a picture:

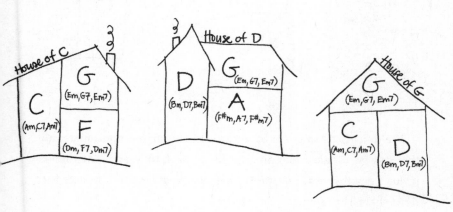

A song in the key of D will have the housemate chords of G and A. When I was writing "The One Who Knows," the chorus had the lines:

> So when they ask how far love goes,
> When my job's done, you'll be the one who knows.

I was looking for something that musically reflected the narrator's outstretched arms, showing how someone wants to extend herself for someone she loves. I didn't have to go far to get that feeling of extension in the music. I recognized that D's housemate, the G chord, also lived in the house of C, so I went over to the house of C to borrow a C chord and easily came back to the house of D (by playing a G, the shared housemate, in this case).

Here's a picture:

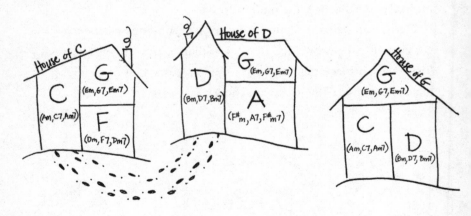

We don't have to come back through the shared housemate, but that can be a logical first attempt to get back to the original house, if that's what we want to do. We can also visit neighbor houses that don't share a housemate, just for kicks.

The mood, the feel, and the narrative will guide our chord choices within each house and help us decide if we want to make an outing to a neighbor's house as well.

"DID I CHANNEL THIS . . . ?"

There comes a moment when we realize our sparkling first inspirations are becoming real songs based on the step-by-step creative decisions we make. As songwriters, we get to decide where our songs are coming from. Did this song emerge from a random place, is it a new slant on the collective unconscious, am I tapping into my psyche's internal logic, or did a supernatural entity bring this song to me?

I know what it's like to worry that I'm not honoring my inspiration's unknowable, sometimes incandescent-feeling source. For almost two weeks now, eight bars of melody have been following me around. I sit and try to find the phrase that does the most justice to this melody, which seems, to me, very pretty.

"This train has come and gone"?

"I have come undone"?

It's easy to get superstitious about how to proceed. Some melodies seem to come to us from another place. They follow us. They haunt us.

When I have a piece of melody in my head, sometimes I feel anxious and tread carefully, just in case the fairies sent it to me. Perhaps the fairy dust will disappear, because the song that's "meant to be" will be replaced by "this thing I wrote when I should have written the other thing."

I pick up the little melody. Is today the day it will be clear? After fifteen minutes, maybe I lay it down gently. Let me try in an hour.

If you feel like you channeled a wonderful fragment of something, but you're wondering, "Now what? I don't want to ruin this," you have my empathy.

That said, you and I have to get past our fear of wrecking a potential thing of beauty and trust that whatever forces brought us to an inspired moment will continue to help us to the end.

Could I, after recording and performing a song, discover a new twist or a better lyric? Yes. Living with the risk that there might be something more perfect is part of our songwriting skill set.

Let's keep going.

NARRATIVE

NARRATION

Once we have followed an inspiration into the first recognizable form of a song, we can also recognize an emerging point of view. We might not have (or ever have) what we'd call a story, but we will have a narrative, even if the final song is seven minutes long and the only lyrics are "Hey, you" at the three-minute mark and "Yeah, you" at the six-minute mark. There is an unfolding, a narration, musically and lyrically. And to guide that narration, we can follow the environmental cues of whatever we have created so far. I call that accumulated song environment the Voice of the song.

THE VOICE OF THE SONG

All is going well as I start a song. A beautiful melody line comes through my head, and it's attached to some words that give me a sense of direction. I've gleaned information from the three or four lines I've made it up to, I have a sense of the ambiance surrounding it, I've made it pretty for myself, I'm getting a sense of what this song will be, and by checking in with "what's up with me?" this song is feeling interesting. Now I can ask a more expansive question that directs how I can continue.

"What is the Voice of this song?"

The Voice is the world, or the overall feel, of the song. The Voice is the tone that will reside throughout the lyrics and music.

The Voice of the song includes the choice of narrator—you, me, it, he, she, they—and the point of view, such as the history of a town told through one specific day. But the Voice doesn't have to have a clear narrator at first. It can actually inform us about who the narrator will be. I started a song with the line "If you're gonna get your heart broke, you better do it just right." I could tell I had a narrator who spoke casually and felt rough around the edges, opting for the abrupt expression "heart broke" over the more flowing "heart broken." She wasn't standing on ceremony, and her humor was mirthless. It was a bad breakup scenario, the one that makes you say, "Wow, this is so awful, it's *perfect*."

The next line became "It's gotta be raining, and you gotta move your stuff that night." Again, I went with the guttural "gotta" over "got to" and the graceless word "stuff." It's the way you'd talk to your friend at a bar. The language helped me know where this narrator was: in the present, feeling emotionally banged up. But she's trying to find her way. She still has some fight in her. I could see the vague shapes of the narrator's world through my memories, such as the apartment stoops of my Boston neighborhood, the streetlamps, the friends who said clueless things in that week after the breakup, and the healing power of old poets at open mics who recited strange but moving things.

The song became "The Blessings," with a consistently tragicomic narrator who stays conversational and a bit sardonic as she looks for signs and portents of happiness in her emotionally split-open world. In the song, any kindness or small mercy is a blessing, but as I proceeded in writing the song, I recognized how the Voice gave the narrator an unsentimental register in which to observe her new reality. She meets poets who offer her coffee, but they note that it's "straight black and very old." The world of this song is full of heartache and unexpected goodness. The poets are in on it, too. They know their coffee is terrible, but their kindness is gold.

The Voice can develop and change. The first priority of writing our songs is to make sure they matter to us, so we can ditch the Voice if it's not speaking to us. It's been done! But if we follow the Voice, as we might choose to speak with an interesting person at a party, staying with the conversation we've started and taking in the whole picture of the story and the storyteller, our exchange will often yield some wonderfully developed, meaningful ideas and revelations.

So many writers at retreats have said they wish they could stop writing silly, sad, angry, or sappy songs. They'll show me a verse and chorus, and we'll recognize that the Voice of the song isn't venturing into the new territory they wanted. Despite the songwriter's wish for a genre shift, the song *wants* to be silly, sad, angry, or sappy, and it's still a meaningful song. The songwriter can decide if they feel more committed to changing genres or to the song that's in front of them.

I usually choose to go where the song wants to go, as opposed to scrapping it to write what I think I should write, and I'll certainly follow the Voice down a few paths before I make any decision. Sometimes the song wants something that is, we realize later, what we wanted, too.

THE SHAPE OF
THE SONG

Here's a crash course in how to build a song. Songs have building blocks:

Verse

Pre-chorus (or "B" part of the verse)

Chorus

Bridge

Tag

Generally, all songs written by a songwriter have these blocks. There are endless ways to arrange them. Most songs don't have all of them. And yes, there are exceptions to songs that have these building blocks, like a chant or the Beatles' "Revolution 9."

How will we arrange these building blocks? The Voice of the song can help us find the right structure.

I was part of a group in which a woman brought a song with a verse and chorus about her city block. After the first chorus, there was a bridge about the street corner in the summer. And then—whoa—the bridge took over! The street corner had a life of its own. She tripled the bridge, added some spoken word and rap, and never came back to a verse or chorus. The narration was unconfined, like the life of the city block itself. The structure went where the action was, and the peripheral world in the bridge—the street corner—became the center of the song.

Meanwhile, Scottish singer-songwriter Donovan's song "Atlantis" is a moody spoken piece set to music, followed by twenty rounds of a chorus that gathers momentum and builds in orchestration as it repeats itself. And that was a hit!

Here's a familiar configuration of blocks for a folk song:

1. Verse

Pre-chorus

Chorus

2. Verse

Pre-chorus

Chorus

Bridge

3. Verse

Pre-chorus

Chorus

Another classic song form is a series of verses that have no chorus but instead go to a pithy end line for each verse or come back to a central tagline, like "Across the wide Missouri" from the traditional song "Shenandoah."

An example of a summary tagline at the end of each verse, derived from traditional blues songs, is Tracy Chapman's song "Give Me One Reason," with taglines such as, "Said, I don't wanna leave you lonely, / You got to make me change my mind."

When I cowrote "Summer Child" with my friend and collaborator Rob Hyman, I knew from the evolving Voice of the song that it would be driven by its chorus.

A melody and words that sounded like a spinning wheel had come into my head.

> *The Summer child is running, Summer child is running,*
> *Summer child is running . . .*

That would be the chorus. I took some summery images I'd gathered when I met up with Rob. Originally, I'd been inspired by a crowd of seven-year-olds at the end of a humid day, creating endless games with the softball, plastic racquets, beach ball, and other things I'd found under my porch. I'd had a rare moment of witnessing the creative, exuberant blur of childhood itself. I knew I wanted to capture that "eternity in a moment" moment, but I also knew that the profundity of my experience couldn't weigh down the fast and playful Voice of the song.

As Rob and I developed the melody, we understood that the images would be fleeting and would work to reinforce the central line, "Summer child is running," which whirred like a perpetual-motion machine.

I knew I wanted to have a bridge that connected these summer scenes to a larger picture, the bigger wheel of the turning seasons.

Okay, so we knew we wanted a lot of choruses, definitely a bridge, and . . . we were off and running with the shape of the song.

We started with a **chorus**, like a celebratory greeting. The summer child is running!

We delved into a **verse** with the details of the stormy, swirling beauty of summer. We started by making verses with eight lines, but that was too much. We were bogging things down. Four lines were short, but they worked.

Another **chorus**!

Another verse? No. We kept it buoyant and went straight to the **bridge**.

The **bridge** would take us on a journey from the cold of winter into the warmth of summer. Could we say it in four lines? Yes. Cool. This song wanted to keep moving.

We added an **instrumental chorus** with Rob's keyboard part. It sounded like running!

We wrote a final **verse** that deepened the wisdom we get from the summer child: time will pass, but we can experience moments of suspended time, of infinity. Very nice . . . but it had to stay within those four lines!

We sang a final **chorus**, varying the words to celebrate the eternal return of the summer child.

And we added a little **tag**: the sun is shining, and the summer child's running again.

Finis.

The Voice of the song gave us our marching orders. A lot of choruses! Short verses! No pre-choruses! The bridge is thoughtful but not too ponderous. Got it!

We can take our time figuring out the best structure for the song. I've learned to trust my friends Trial and Error. Let the Voice guide the shape. And, if a certain structure works, it might influence what the Voice will become or change into. That can happen, too.

TRANSITIONS BETWEEN THE BUILDING BLOCKS OF SONGS

The Voice of the song can help guide how our verse goes into the chorus, or whether there is a chorus, and where (and whether) to add a bridge or a tag. Musically, when we go from block to block, we'll usually go to one of the chord's housemates, or to another of the housemate's "moods," like the minor or minor seventh, just as a story will change moods as we tell it.

I've always heard that the chorus should be a little higher than the verse, but plenty of times, the Voice has led me to make the chorus lower. If a narrator is mourning something, the chorus might hunker down melodically.

The "Spring Street" verse starts in the key of G with four lines that muse on feeling uncomfortable with my friends' breezy assurance that I can pick up and leave a relationship. It's straightforward. We're starting with the start, stating the conflict at hand. So, I start with the root chord, the one chord, the G.

In the next four lines, also called the pre-chorus, I'm asking if I can move out and move away. It's like I'm taking something farther up a path to get a better view of the situation. The "questioning" tone goes to the higher housemate chord, the C, as does the melody.

The chorus is a declaration of incredulity. It starts with the lines, "I can't believe what they're saying. / They're saying I can leave tonight." Here I return to the root, the G, but with a higher melody. It's like I've returned to the original place of "I can't believe my friends are telling me I can leave," but now, with the higher notes (almost an octave higher), I'm saying, "I CAN'T BELIEVE THEY'RE TELLING ME THIS!"

The Voice of this song led me to this structure. I'd been sitting in a café in New York City, thinking about a corner apartment on Spring Street that had potted plants in all the windows. Someone had a life that looked so easy and achievable. I wanted that. My friends who lived in the city told me I should come on down. The phrase "Start over on Spring Street" came into my mind. What would it mean if I just showed up in Massachusetts and said, "Bought an apartment in New York. See ya." I could just do that. Wait . . . COULD I JUST DO THAT?? Hence, the structure of the song.

On the other hand, in my anthem about coming out of clinical depression, "After All," the chorus is only a little higher, brighter, and less wordy than the verse. The narrator is arriving at revelations slowly and tentatively, like she's putting down a foot and testing the ground before she puts any weight on it. The transition from verse to chorus reflects her caution. The chorus can't just come jumping out of a cake.

In another song, "Magical Thinking," I bleed the verse right into the chorus. The narrator is filling up all the space with words, not leaving room for someone to interject and tell her she is irrational. She knows she is. She's steamrolling, not going up and down melodically or making any distinct breaks for the chorus. It's like she's saying, "Let me get all of this out before I lose my thread or get misunderstood."

All of these are examples of how we can feel our way through transitions between the building blocks in our songs.

MAKING A MAP OF
SONGS AND LINES

We can map our songs as they start to take shape. It's common to identify lines of a song with letters. The names of building blocks— verse, pre-chorus, tag, chorus—can also give us a map to follow. Lines that rhyme or that occupy the same space in every verse will have the same letters, like this:

> Verse A: The cloud will form a crown
> B: Circling the rocky mountaintop
> A: Telling us the rain is coming soon
> B: As we sail the river up and down
> Chorus C: The Storm King has borne the seasons all
> D: Worn them upon his brow
> C: He guides the watchful boats below
> D: I am the Storm King now.

Each line will generally have its own length, as well. I was interested to find that James Keelaghan shared my trick of writing down spaces to show the number of syllables I have to work within a line.

I was writing a bridge in which a child was reciting facts about hummingbirds. In the Voice of the song, the child speaks in excited bursts of information. I wrote this down:

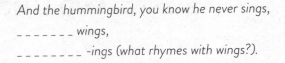

> *And the hummingbird, you know he never sings,*
> *_ _ _ _ _ _ _ wings,*
> *_ _ _ _ _ _ _ _ -ings (what rhymes with wings?).*

I could put in a few extra syllables if I phrased them right and if the words flowed (some vowels and consonants flow more smoothly than others), but these spaces were helpful estimates for what I had to work with. I ended up writing:

> *And the hummingbird, y'know he never sings,*
> *The humming comes from his flapping wings,*
> *And he only likes the sweetest things . . .*

If we've got a metaphor or analogy we're dying to use, these place-holder spaces can tell us how much room we have, or if we have enough room at all.

THE DANCE OF THE MESSAGE AND THE FORM

We've had the inspiration and gathered the clues, figured out some chords or the ambiance around the melody, and felt around for things that are fascinating to us. We've started to see where the Voice has been leading us, and we've gotten a general sense of structure. We've explored things loosely, letting serendipity, the existing information in the song, and our own subconscious ideas become a part of the process. We might even have a rudimentary map of its structure. How do we continue to hold the reins and continue to write our songs?

When classical guitarist and professor Jorge Torres heard me talk about songwriting, he said, "So basically, the ear leads the song, and the song leads the ear?" Yes, each can lead the other: the form of the song, musically and lyrically, can inform the message of the song. The message of the song, lyrically and musically (because music delivers a message, too!), can guide the form. And even better than that, each can *help* the other along. I love the way Jorge identified the "ear": songwriting is a hearing and listening process, even if we're not listening with our literal ears. We can get an overall sense of things from what we're *hearing*, or we can *listen* closely for information.

From a *form* standpoint, for instance, we can hear how a newly discovered rhythm sounds like a galloping horse and decide that the young suitor in our song will feel like a knight, using chivalric language, calling his bicycle his steed and his girlfriend "My lady."

On the other hand, from a *message* standpoint, we can listen to the lyrics, which are the thoughts of an earnest young suitor, and decide to underscore his knight-like chivalry by creating a rhythm that gallops like a horse. Form and message, message and form. We can allow them both to in*form* one another and the song we're writing.

STARTING WITH FORM

As we start to follow the inspirations of our songs, we are establishing the feel, the rhythm, the register of the language, and/or the cadences. In that discovery process, we may find ourselves exploring the form for a while before we get a clear picture of the message. We might not know what we're writing about. That's more than okay. It can be exciting. If I'm working on something and I don't know where the form is leading, I'll try to move around, literally, moving my hands, my neck, or my whole body, just to let myself feel the possibilities instead of just thinking my way to the lyrical message.

Perhaps a line that's popped into my head is generating melodic and lyrical lines with no story or even a discernible narrative.

"Keep it in the air, YEAH! Keep it in the air, YEAH!" leads to "All my friends are there, YEAH! All of them are there! YEAH!" and then comes, "Playing in the sun, we're playing in the sun." The form of the song is bouncy, percussive, fun. The repetition gives it the feel of a punchy sports cheer. I'll go with that form for a while until I finally realize that my narrator is on a beach playing volleyball. A meaning can manifest itself from out of that setting. The meaning might be very form based, that is, the song will simply be a rowdy testament to the joy of playing on the beach. Or it might become more message based, with a story and a set of characters, like, "We fell in love, playing in the sand. Why did Chad leave us all for Hollywood-land?"

When I wrote "The Business of Things," I heard the lines "It's a cold, cold time; it's a cold, cold time . . ." in my head for a few days. I recognized that it was a waltz with a minor-chord feel. I waltzed around with that rhythm and the chilliness of those words. I kept on thinking of the song "Moon River": a lighthearted melody with a wistful narrative. The next lyric I heard was "And it makes me wonder if I'll ever forget . . ." Forget what? I stayed with the form and the feel. I let those lines play in my head for a while until the next lyric appeared: "How cold I, how cold I . . ." Okay, I've discovered my inner coldness. Callousness, perhaps? Keep dancing. And then the last line, ". . . and the world can be."

It was only after I had moved around with this melancholic, waltzy feeling that I asked myself, "What's up with me? How can this relate to what feels interesting to me?" and the answer was "Business breakups." I had a sudden recognition that a recent "business breakup" was very emotional for me and something I wanted to explore in this song. We write a lot of songs about leaving partners and even friends, but I was feeling heartbroken over a relationship that the world had called "just business." The lazy-river, sad sweetness of the melody underscored the feelings that gave rise to the themes and then the rest of the song. The song had minor chords as well as "seventh" chords that held the pensively sad feelings that I experienced musically before I explored them lyrically.

FOLLOWING THE MESSAGE

"Form and content" is a common word pairing, but in songwriting, I prefer the word "message" to "content." Contents fill a container. A message is a missive, a communiqué, even a manifesto. We can decode it, discover it on an attic wall, or find it in a bottle.

What is the message? What do we want to say? What do we *really* want to say? This is what I ask myself. For even my lightest songs, I go on a mission of searching: soul-searching, researching (re-searching), and searching for meaning.

I ask myself the following questions:

Where did I go? Where did I *really* go? What happened? What *really* happened? How did it feel, and how did it *really* feel?

As we saw in the preceding chapter, we can reside in the pure forms of sound and feeling for a while before we start to zone in on the lyrical message of our song, so these "message" questions can come before, after, or during an exploration of form. Also, the form of the song can be called the musical message, so these "where, what, and how" questions can be asked musically as well. We might put bright, major chord under the words "I'm so happy," only to realize that what *really* happened will sound more honest with a minor-chord tinge of regret.

WHERE DID I GO?

As the Voice of the song emerges, so will a world with its own landscape and feel. By taking an actual journey to that world, whether it's into our backyard or onto an imaginary planet, we get to collect some useful illustrative details, and we often get a better sense of what the song is *about*. We can also cast about that landscape for things we can pick up and put down as we see what serves the song: What do I want from this old basement, with its workbench, kitty litter box, old freezer, and boiler that looks like the belly of a giant robot? What do I want from my summer camp, with its lake, tennis courts, pine trees, camp uniforms, and midnight run-ins with spiders and skunks in the outhouse?

One time I had to go spend some time with the moon. For a week or so, all I had in my head was the four-note phrase "Calling the moon." I gathered the clues. It was in waltz time. It had a narrator who was "calling" out for answers. I imagined that the song would have to do with feeling out of touch with some kind of "natural" state of being, based on my own recent sense of estrangement from the natural world, a by-product of constant touring.

I drove to the local community garden one night and watched the moon for a while. I made observations.

- When the moon came out from behind a cloud, a beautiful expanse of fields and trees seemed to *manifest* in front of me.
- The moonlight seemed like it was painted on the landscape.
- The moonlight felt gentle and unjudgmental, but it also seemed impassive as it rose in the sky.

I sensed that something was happening as I sat in my car. The moon affected how I saw things and how I felt. In this moment, for instance, if I were to shed my vanity and aggressive striving, this nonglaring moonlight would provide an emotional oasis in which I could value my sensitivity and quiet self. I was starting to discover what this "calling the moon" could be about.

I explored additional themes and metaphors as I sat and watched. There were hits and misses as I speculated about different aspects of the moon.

- Was there something relevant to the song in the moon's symmetrical shape? No.
- Craters? No.
- Phases? No.
- Greek moon goddess? No.
- Moon landing? No.
- Tidal forces? Ah. Yes.

The forces of the moon influence the ocean tides, powerfully, yet invisibly. As an artist, I could relate to that unseen magnetic force. The influence of art on the tides of civilization seems as improbable as a moon influencing the motion of the sea. The moon is far from the wave that crashes on a rock. The artist will never know where peace reigns instead of war thanks to the power of symphonies, plays, and poetry (and songs).

Thus, by sitting with the actual moon for a while, I understood that I was searching for more than just a sense of connection with nature. I was looking for emotional and spiritual respite in the moon's reflected light, and I also renewed my faith in the powers we cannot see.

I remembered that, like the moon,

> I know what it's worth,
> To tug at the seas and illumine the earth.

WHERE DID I *REALLY* GO?

After we've staked out where we went, one thing that will help us write our songs and legitimize them to others is to ask, "Where did I *really* go?" For example, most people expect that a place of worship is where we look for God, but perhaps we'll have a narrator who went to that place because he had an illicit crush on his cousin, he wanted to hear the music, or he realized that he loved those powdery lemon cookies after the service. Where we really go is a very personal destination, and it's worth exploring without judgment.

We can also play with form as a way to experience where we really went. Maybe a song we're writing is ragged and loose with only barely rhyming rhymes and not a lot of specific imagery. If where I went, emotionally, was a raggedly loose mood with more colors and feelings than tangible objects, then the form and message of the song will support that I really went to that nebulous "place" and brought back this song.

Art's gift to the listener, as well as the writer, is its ability to show what we perceive, not just report on things or skim the surface. Thus, it can be helpful in songwriting to look around and inside a "place" and see what aspects and nuances of the terrain have truly defined our experience there.

When I was writing about Berkeley, California, I went back to the summer when I lived there, and then to more than twenty-five years of visits on tour. I collected a range of images and thought about where they fit in the emotional, thematic picture I wanted to draw.

When I lived there, I always saw the colors. There were flowers everywhere. There were tie-dyed shirts, skirts, and dresses. At twenty years old, I heard about the coming Revolution from organizers at the Communist Youth Center. I learned about the California law system from a guy who carried discarded law books around in his grocery cart. I entertained a multiverse of ideas about politics, spirituality, art, and existence itself. Also, there was this amazing coffee drink I discovered called a "latté" served in a pint glass that I'd drink in a café. It cost two dollars.

When I went back over the years, I watched the city changing. I collected up all the walks and talks I could remember from those years, like visiting the Pacifica radio station and walking with one of the fund-raising volunteers through a eucalyptus forest, doing a wild concert with Joan Baez, drinking (now four-dollar) lattés at the original Peet's Coffee and Tea, and watching the homes get fancier as the homeless population got more angry.

I could have written about a place that got more gentrified and sold out its deepest hippie values, but I realized that where I *really* went, I could always find that old Berkeley, the one where I'd lived in 1987 (and it still felt like 1967). I *really* went to a place that still held a space for its old self and my old self, too. The communist bookstore is still there, the purveyors of tie-dye and candles are still odd dreamers, and I am still, somewhere, the idealistic romantic whose erstwhile, impossible relationship with an impossible person still makes some sense when seen in the glow of Berkeley's lavender light.

When "we go there" and show that "we really went there," we recognize and have the opportunity to capture the unique feelings and aspects of a space (or metaphoric space), and in so doing, we offer a valuable gift, the gift of honest witness, that may inspire true recognition in our listeners, as well.

WHAT HAPPENED?

When I have a lead on "where I went," seeing which details are interesting and relevant to the song, sometimes the scene becomes a freeze frame. Okay, this is where I went. Where does the song go now? I can see and sense the terrain, but what's going to happen next? This is when I ask the simple question, "Well . . . what happened?"

What was the sequence of events, and what was the narrator's experience of the event?

When I was writing the song "After All," about having depression in my twenties, I kept on going back to *what happened*.

I'd gotten the first lines,

> Go ahead, push your luck, find out how much love the world
>   can hold,
> Once upon a time I had control and reined my soul in tight.

Now what?

What happened when I became depressed? I felt paralyzed and frozen.

And . . . ? Every bad mood lasted for days.

And . . . ? My friends told me I needed help, and not very kindly.

Then . . . ? I went to therapy.

Then . . . ? I found out more of my family's history, among other
things, and even the weird parts helped me feel better.

And then what . . . ? My life turned from a black-and-white
photo to a color one.

And . . . ? When I felt better, "I" was *me*, not "the embodiment of
everything shameful and bad in the universe."

And . . . ? I still had ups and downs, but they were not engulfed
by waves of shame.

And . . . ? I was a better friend and girlfriend, because I was
ready to hear what people said, positive and negative, without fearing a descent back into depression.

Asking myself what happened helped me understand the progression of the verses (from rock bottom to the surface, from fear to courage, from shame to dignity), the kind of language I would use (poetic
but not too flowery), and the ultimate meaning of the song for me.

> **First verse:** *what depression felt like*
> **Second verse:** *therapy, finding out my story*
> **Third verse:** *coming back to life, with its everyday risks and
> rewards*

As I understood the form and message and started to write the
verses, I asked the next important question: What *really* happened?

WHAT *REALLY* HAPPENED?

This is the moment when we sit in a chair, or move our bodies around, and focus in on how it *really* was, and we allow those feelings to formulate in two ways. One is to identify our experiences honestly. The other is to find the metaphors of those experiences, if we're going to include metaphors.

For instance, as I was writing my song about depression, I remembered that one of the only reasons I stayed alive was that I felt I couldn't abandon an equally depressed friend. I didn't want to live or die. That was what *really* happened: I was in limbo, much as I'd love to say that my first step out of depression was joyful and unambivalent.

Sometimes I observed a depth of beauty around me that was both painful and euphoric. That *really* happened: reality could get distorted, sometimes in beautiful ways. I'd get caught up in a highly stimulating, fast-moving sensory world that felt like a high, though my reveries were accompanied by a sense of profound unworthiness. Coming out of depression was a mix of feeling more ordinary and, paradoxically, more worthy.

I started to join those true-feeling experiences with corresponding metaphors.

When I had those ten-day, or one-month, bad moods, what was that like? It was like going through a repetition of coldness and grayness while other people seemed to emerge and move on from breakups, bad grades, or humiliating interactions. It was like a machine, a winter machine that you go through, and then you catch your breath, and winter starts again. Yes, that's how it felt. And it was worse than that. Everyone *else* seemed to make it through to the spring.

That's what it really felt like, and those are the lines I wrote.

At every step, I asked myself what happened and then what *really* happened until I both remembered and identified how it *really* was to leave that depression and suicidal ideation behind. Simultaneously, I started to find the language and metaphors that would express what really happened. For instance, at the end of this crazy depression, when I discovered that I deserved to live, I felt like *life* chose *me* after all.

And that's what I wrote, too.

HOW DOES IT FEEL? HOW DOES IT *REALLY* FEEL?

When a person is in therapy, sometimes that person will start to cry. Tears are like manna from heaven for most therapists, who will often say, "Stay there. What is *happening* right now?" Tears show that we are experiencing our emotional reality.

Likewise, there can be a feeling that governs a song-in-formation. Some songs will start with a feeling. In fact, sometimes the feeling will be the most definitive guide. We feel our way along. We can give language to a feeling by asking, as we ask where we've gone and what has happened, "What is the color, the mood, the emotion here?"

It can be a very vague feeling, like "melancholy," "giddy," or "confrontational."

The first time Jill Sobule and I sat down to work on "FM Radio," we only wrote two lines, but we had an amazing time going back and looking at Billboard charts from when we were preteens in the seventies. Jill, in a reverie, said she remembered getting a sleek black bicycle. She duct-taped a transistor radio to the handlebars and rode through the streets of a Denver suburb, hands on the handlebars, head lowered, eyes up, cruising like she was on a motorcycle.

Then we talked about public pools, where the girls, high on pheromones, Coppertone, and women's lib, catcalled the handsome lifeguards and lip-synched songs on the radio. We remembered how we posed and how we danced in our bathing suits. We jumped off diving boards (which have long since been condemned). We became confident as we tried on different confident personalities looped through the celebrities of FM radio.

From these feelings—because by now we had entered that whole sense-world—we ended up getting the first verse, as well as lines like "yelled 'Barracuda!' off the high-dive" ("Barracuda" is a song by Heart), and fan-worshipping references to Patty Hearst, Lou Reed, Jackson Browne, and Queen. We followed our feelings, and the important details came to the surface.

If you took a movie of that actual time in the seventies, you might see a flailing bunch of awkward, insecure kids with sunburns wearing bathing suits that are pilled up from lying on the cement. Those teenagers wouldn't look so pumped up and self-assured. But the feeling Jill and I summoned up, the joyful romance with FM radio, was the truly felt emotion that drove the song.

"WRITING WHAT YOU KNOW"

What is the relationship between "really going" to a place and the adage to "write what you know"?

A cadet at West Point Military Academy, dressed in desert camouflage fatigues, came to my songwriting clinic and asked about this recommendation to "write what you know." I said I understood the expression, but that I didn't expect her to write only about being at West Point. In fact, being at such an elite military institution might bring up themes of mortality, civilization, sacrifice, character, and spirituality that would benefit from being explored through other conduits than the academy itself.

If, in exploring the importance of knowing her own moral compass, this cadet felt a song coming on about the quiet force of contemplation, perhaps the narrator of her song would be a sixteenth-century nun. The writer might want to go to a church, on campus or off campus, or to the Cloisters Museum down the Hudson River from West Point, or to a library with picture books of paintings by El Greco. She might read a book about Saint Teresa of Avila or watch a movie about her. She might take some long walks in an arboretum.

There are many ways to go to a place, even *really* go to a place, poetically, no matter what our academy or uniform. If that writer recognizes, in the metaphoric space of her own construction, what really happened, how it really felt, and what its unique qualities were, then she will be writing what she knows.

WHEN WE HAVEN'T GONE, EXPERIENCED, *OR* FELT WHAT WE'RE WRITING ABOUT

I recently heard a song about a small-town girl in an abusive marriage. I knew the writer well enough to know that she had not grown up in that small town, nor had she, from the vagueness of her descriptions in the song, truly, empathically, gone to a place from which she could narrate with any authenticity.

There are a few problems with these "ripped from the headlines" songs that stay at a nonempathetic distance, no matter how personal they sound or how *sympathetic* the writer is about the topic.

The audience members who have experienced and felt this thing won't believe the song, and they might even end up distrusting the writer in general. When we stay on the surface of observation, sometimes we miss the nuances that true observers or researchers can offer. I could write a song about a person escaping an abusive husband and searching for—I'd be guessing—a place to go, assistance from friends, and the love of a good partner. When I spoke with an advocate for domestic abuse survivors, however, she said that a surprising number of women want counseling opportunities for the men who abused them. I hadn't seen that coming.

Songwriters don't have to get every detail right. And chances are that if we don't "really go there," and we offer a picture with no insights or evidence of personal connection, a song will simply and innocently go by the wayside. But there is a reason that I've loved leading retreats that are called "Writing a Song that Matters." The process of getting ourselves into the shoes of our narrators, even if we don't hit a bull's-eye, can yield more meanings, for our listeners and ourselves, than writing what we think the world wants to hear or writing to point fingers and visit judgment upon others from a distance. No one wants to hear the ballad of a two-pack-a-day, hard-living divorcée, written by a twelve-year-old. Even when I went to Nashville and sat in writing rooms with seasoned hook-devising, chart-topping writers, the first thing we did was to talk about what felt interesting and important and *real* to us personally.

STARTING A SONG
WITH A TOPIC

I've written a lot so far about the ways that we can fan the sparks of inspiration that come to us.

Sometimes we want to, or are asked to, write about specific things. Personally, when I've been asked to write a song about a specific idea or person, I spend some time walking around with the suggested topic and seeing if something comes to me as a poetic reality. If nothing comes to me, I decline the invitation. I bristle when I hear that songwriters "should" write songs "about" particular things. I want to write songs, not lectures and encyclopedia entries, and I can't will the poetic vantage point, with all its dimensions and perspectives, into existence on demand.

But I do like to rise to the occasion of writing for my times. The problem is that concepts, causes, and honorable personages can be as hard to engage, from a songwriting perspective, as a locked file cabinet. The contents of the drawer have all the material I want, but I need to find the right key to open it. Once I find something that strikes me emotionally, poetically, and personally, I can unlock the drawer and take on all that information. When I find the silver key, I open a drawer that can be filled with rich and complex information, but now it's not foreboding, because I've found a way in and I know which files to pull.

In the early days of the 2020 pandemic, I had no idea how to process things personally, let alone how to write a song about it. I felt overwhelmed. I processed the situation as fast as I could, which, for me, means the speed of a horse-drawn covered wagon filled with heavy furniture. Every new connection I make tends to jostle a whole pile of other connections.

But then I saw a picture of the Himalayas that the residents of a northern Indian town could see for the first time in decades. There had been an abrupt cessation of pollution that cleared their view. I knew this photograph was my key into writing about the pandemic.

I'm still working on the song. I asked my Buddhist songwriting buddy Jim Infantino what he thought, and immediately we started talking about mountains in meditation metaphors, in the spiritual world, and in the natural world. And then we talked about the relationship between inner and outer worlds. Is the newly smog-free air like the clear mind? When the smog returns, will the narrator get off her meditation pillow more often and advocate for clean air, or will she return to the "sacred mountain" in her mind?

Stay tuned. Now that I've found the key and gotten into the drawer, I'm sorting through information to see what belongs and doesn't belong in this song, and I'm very excited about it.

And by the way, if you're asked to write a song for a cause or an event, and the key to the file drawer is not to be found, you can use a song that's already been written (there are thousands of them, literally!) or adapt lyrics of an existing song to fit the occasion.

WRITING ABOUT HISTORY

Songs have themes that guide the narrative, even when we're writing about nonfictional historic events. A song that's based on a historical event will still have to honor the aspects of the event that are relevant to those themes. History happens, and art is an interpretation of that history.

Sarah came to our retreat and talked about her Oklahoma-themed songs for an upcoming record. She held up a small folder of papers, explaining that there was an equivalent folder of research for each song. We ended up searching through each historical event to find the thematic connections in their stories.

In her song about Mickey Mantle, she had a beautiful, simple chorus, "A father's love for his son. A son's love for his father." This chorus provided Sarah's silver key to how she would both depict Mantle and show how his story was somehow a uniquely Oklahoman tale. That was a challenge!

In the first verse we learned that Mantle's father did baseball drills with his son every night after work. Sarah hadn't yet mentioned that his father worked in the mines, and we agreed that putting in this detail would make the geography (a little) more specific and emphasize the sacrifice the father was making by doing something so physically demanding after a day of exhausting work.

Mickey Mantle had his demons. Sarah said there were stories of his fraught relationship with his father as well as reports of excess and crisis in Mantle's adult life. It was tempting to tell the most vivid, shocking parts of Mantle's history, but if Sarah was going to bring them up, they would have to be in the context of the father-son story, according to what we'd discussed.

Sarah mentioned that every time a siren went off in Mantle's town, it meant someone had died or been hurt at the mines. We thought she could put that detail in a bridge to help explain the reasons for the father's tough love. Playing catch every night meant saving his son from being that monthly siren blast. Her Mickey Mantle story now had to do with an Oklahoman family finding a better future. We were being true to the thematic crux of Sarah's project and song.

History presents us with big dossiers of information. Sarah had read more than enough to know many public and private stories about Mickey Mantle. Her extensive knowledge could have been a hindrance at first—so many details to choose from, and so many dramatic distractions! But the history she gathered was ultimately a big help. When she knew what kind of father-son relationship she wanted at the heart of her song, she could pick up and discard details, choosing the best ones to heighten the themes of an Oklahoman baseball icon's tough-love boyhood.

THAT PERFECT SPOT BETWEEN THE GENERAL AND SPECIFIC

Isn't it strange how we connect to specific experiences that are completely different from our own? One song's narrator, a farmer hacking away at the red-clay dirt of Virginia as he grieves dear Betsy's departure, forms an empathic bond with a teenage listener yanking weeds at the country club as he quietly sobs over his breakup with Sara. And strangely, it's the *specifics* that somehow bring out the universality of the grief over Betsy and Sara.

Specific details can give a sense of place, as well as a freshness, beauty, and credibility, that brings our stories to life for our listeners. Listeners who don't know the street names, hair colors, and old cars can still make vivid connections.

What details shall we keep when we've done the work of going to a particular time and place to get our songs? Here's the paramount thing to remember: a song is based on themes. We will choose details that reinforce both the Voice and the themes of our song. A song is the opposite of the proverbial police officer who says, "Just the facts, ma'am."

We'll ask ourselves which parts of a narrator's life fill out the picture in a song. What observations will connect to the themes of the overall story? That question might lead to some difficult choices.

Just as we saw how a songwriter pared the many details of Mickey Mantle's life down to her song's central themes, we will have to make decisions when we write about history, including our own personal histories.

Perhaps a songwriter's recently deceased father has left an old wallet on his dresser. The wallet is stuffed with tollbooth receipts, discount cards for three garden-supply stores, and a few crumpled dollar bills. The writer can use these true details to illustrate his dad's frugality or bring out other pecuniary themes. But if the themes of the song are more about the father as seen through his love of animals, the writer's beautifully observed moment of going through the wallet will probably be irrelevant. The coat hook with seven well-worn dog leashes, on the other hand, will serve the narrative. Letting go of that wallet will be hard for the writer, but the themes will dictate the edit.

Specific names can add contours as well as a sense of connection. Ideally, these names parallel the themes of the songs with a happy synchronicity. If I'm writing a love song that unfolds over a summer at a house on Shadow Lake, and the romance happens to live in the *shadows,* fore*shadows* a future, or provides cooling shade from the harsh heat of our lives, then I'll probably keep the specific name. If the lake is named for what it looks like, Pig Butt, I guarantee that the specific name will go.

We can also use a true name that sounds interesting and beautiful but doesn't march hand-in-hand with the themes of the song, like Birch Street or Wheelbarrow Lane. A name that doesn't correspond with the exact themes of the song can be refreshingly . . . real. But the audience ear will inevitably be listening for themes, so something that is completely at odds with our thematic environment can be a distraction.

A song is like a stage. Everything signifies something. That's why actors are told to pick something up if it accidentally drops. The audience will see a fallen red hair ribbon in that hyperassociative, fictional space called the stage and start connecting it, metaphorically, with the rest of the images they see.

On the stage of a song, mellifluous names like Lilypad Pond, Helen Jackson Boulevard, and Winter Road can go with the flow of a song. We just have to remember that Lilypad Pond *might* conjure up images of frogs and the countryside, the mind might ask who "Helen Jackson" was and wonder if she represents something in the story, and Winter Road might be associated with images of a road that gets icy and treacherous in the cold weather.

The best example of fortuitous, synchronistic specificity I encountered was at a retreat where William and I were sitting with his song about struggling up and down a hill in his college town. It was a coming-of-age song. We agreed that somehow if we had a specific name of a street or a park, it would give the song more character. There were a lot of abstract insights in the song, so we wanted to ground the narrative with something to show that this terrain was traveled in real time.

We were casting about for a beautiful or interesting name from the real place where William had been. Even Maple Street would have worked. Suddenly, William remembered the name of the hill itself. It was called Revelation Hill. We had a moment where we considered if Revelation Hill sounded too fictional! But we realized it was perfect. We were able to locate the narrator within this difficult daily journey he took, toughing it out through all the seasons, showing the revelations that combine real exertion with mental striving. The song came into focus before our eyes, allowing us to strengthen our empathy for a young student whose revelations were born of the challenges to the body, mind, and soul as he literally trudged up the hill to school.

In my own songwriting experience, I worried that writing a song about the Hudson River, with its unique landscape, would make sense only around New York. This was not the case. I sing it everywhere, even with its specific references to the George Washington Bridge and Harlem (less majestic-sounding touchstones, like Turkey Hill, didn't make the cut, however). I can practically hear my Alaskan, Texan, and Floridian audiences connecting with the story because my experience springs so *specifically* from my own beloved Hudson Valley. It's as if the place where I *really* went spurs their associations of where they *really* went. Whether it's Thunder Road, Penny Lane, Electric Avenue, or Sesame Street, if our specific details correlate to the feel and story of the song, we can trust our listeners will go to their own equivalent place, emotionally, and feel strangely closer to a Someone living Somewhere than to Anyone living Anywhere.

HARNESSING THE METAPHORS OF SPACE AND TIME

How we write about time and space can be elastic and poetically evocative in two ways: how we experience them and how we measure them.

We can experience time and space subjectively, such as "living a lifetime in a moment." In the song "February," I wrote, "February was so long that it lasted into March." That's how time felt to me.

The other way we communicate a poetic time-space reality is in the units we use to measure it. When the narrator of the song "Road Buddy" was excited about the new things he'd see on a road trip from Spokane, Washington, to Phoenix, Arizona, the distance of the trip was measured as "from where the moss grows up the trees to where the dirt is rusty red."

Giving a personal scale to time and space reveals a personal landscape and often sheds light on the human experience in general.

As an exercise, let's say two people are across a twenty-foot room from one another. How can we use time and space to illustrate the relationship between them?

If a narrator says the distance is "wide as a winter lake," we hear that the span of twenty feet *feels* like a quarter of a mile, and it's not gauged in yards or meters, but instead with the measuring unit of one desolate, frozen chasm of water.

If someone feels like they're about to be trapped by the other person, the distance can be "a lasso throw" away. If it's love at first sight, one person might hop across "a mere three clouds" to stand next to the other.

As I write songs, I don't set out to measure time and space metaphorically. The subjective measurements usually come up naturally when I am asking the questions "What really happened?" and "How did it really feel?" Often my experience will reflect my subjective perception of time and space, and I will enjoy the imagistic, poetic freedom I have in the expression of my narrator's felt reality, measured in anything from tree rings to planetary epochs to the span of an average temper tantrum.

FOCUSING TIME AND SPACE

When I was growing up, I had an old microscope in my room. I loved how smoothly the brass eyepiece tube would move up and down as I adjusted the focus on a bird feather, a flower petal, or a dead fly.

If we put a song on the appropriately named "viewing stage" of the microscope, we get to look in, turn the knob, and bring it into the focus we want, hazy or sharp, cellular or panoramic.

The Voice of the song can guide how detailed versus how broad we want to go.

In one song, I'll enter a room, noticing every detail as I go. I turn the doorknob, step onto the thick Persian carpet, cross the room silently, carefully pull out black gloves and a flashlight and a velvet bag, lean into the safe, spin the dial, and listen for the combination, tumbler by tumbler, until the door cracks open.

This could be the first verse of a song called "How I Plan to Steal Your Heart." The step-by-step precision is essential to the Voice of this song.

But if the song is called "Ghost of an Outlaw," we'll skip that whole intimate thieving experience and move in broader strokes of time.

I was a safecracker,
I was a crook,
In and out like the match from a little matchbook!

We will measure time in seconds if we want to play up the suspense, proceeding across that thick carpet. But if we want to lament the days of the old-fashioned outlaw, with a bizarre code of conduct and love of sleeping on the desert floor (or whatever makes outlaws happy), we might want to . . . pick up the pace. Time and steps will be measured and counted by what kind of story we want to tell.

TELL THE STORY AND NOTICE HOW IT'S HEARD

It's no surprise that James Keelaghan, who has written many epic story songs, is interested in the art of storytelling in general. He suggests that when we have a story to tell, we should tell it to different groups of friends and see how the listeners respond to different parts of the narrative.

Not all of us have that many friends, and we might not have the patience to hear how a narrative percolates through the many strata of receivers.

However, James's suggestion to watch the effects of our narration and observe the high points and nuances that emerge consistently through many tellings helps to define how we'll recount the event. The song is both the story we tell and how we tell it, whether we call the result fiction, creative nonfiction, or poetic reality.

James's song "Cold Missouri Waters" tells the story of elite firefighting "smokejumpers" in western Montana who arrive by plane to put out raging wildfires. R. Wagner "Wag" Dodge describes how he has led his group into the fire. When the fire changes course, the crew is in danger. Dodge creates a fire around himself to cut the fuel source of the approaching blaze. He encourages his men to join him, but they don't believe him. He is one of a few survivors.

James had to decide where to join the immediacy of the plot with themes of the story. James's narrator, "Dodge," the crew chief, begins the song from his deathbed in a hospital, years after the fire. Dodge will tell the story of "thirteen crosses high above the cold Missouri waters." Right from the first verse, we start with high stakes: life, death, and biblical New Testament metaphors.

Then he goes from the grand theme to the moment-by-moment description of the event. The smokejumpers are called to put out a wildfire started by lightning. James uses words that are specific to Dodge's profession, putting us right in his shoes.

> Picked the drop zone, C-47 comes in low
> Feel the tap upon your leg that tells you go . . .

We can guess what a drop zone is and what the tap is. I never knew if C-47 was a plane or a marked-off quadrant! It's a plane. But it didn't matter if I knew. Dodge knew.

These details heighten the themes of loss in this song. Dodge knows his stuff. His instincts lead him, correctly, to build a fire inside a fire, just as they've led him to direct the jump into the fire scene with an intuitive "tap" on the leg. His men don't follow him, an all too understandable, yet completely tragic, mutiny against their trusted leader.

These details are also great yarn-spinning. We lean in as if we're sitting with James at a campfire.

We follow the story of that one day, right up to the carrying of bodies to the river, and then we zoom back up to the big picture with Dodge on his deathbed again, reflecting that now he will "join" the other smokejumpers.

The song is based on a three-hundred-page nonfiction novel called *Young Men and Fire*, by Norman MacLean. There are many plot points beyond the event itself, from lawsuits and recrimination to modern fire policies based on what happened that day in Mann Gulch.

How did James distill all of those pages into five verses with no choruses? Maybe James told fifty people the story, or maybe he took some long walks and followed his own narrative intuition. Either way, the song strikes a powerful balance between an exciting plot with intimately observed details and universal perspectives with crushing emotional lessons.

In my mind, I see James telling the story to real and invisible people, learning that the parts of the story that made the most impact were the event itself and the end-of-life lessons from it, not the parts about litigation or firefighting innovations. There's also a twist in one of the last lines. The dying Dodge says, "I'll join them now, those who left me long before." He experiences both the survivor's anguish and the frustration that their distrust meant that they "left" him behind. Whenever I get to this part of the song, this intimation of feeling both guilty and betrayed, I'm grateful that James included this paradox, and I don't quite know why, any more, perhaps, than James will know why a person's eyebrows went up or down when he first relayed the story.

So how did he do? I was onstage with him the first time I heard the song, and I was completely rapt, as was the audience. "Cold Missouri Waters" has been recorded by at least five other artists (including me, with my friends Lucy Kaplansky and Richard Shindell). Also, when Wag Dodge's widow met James, she said, "You got it right."

SHOWING, NOT TELLING?

Well-chosen words and images can help us do that thing we're told to do: "show, don't tell." Yet "show, don't tell" never helped me become a better songwriter. I finally figured out why that admonition rang false for me. Showing is a *way* of telling, and telling can be a *way* of showing. The Voice of the song will dictate how to communicate accordingly.

Illustrious descriptions and metaphors can lend beauty and precision to our stories. Words that are consistent with the narration, whether they're choppy, flowing, or "clickety-clack," can move the story along with seamless grace. But if I write a line that just says, "She was really unhappy," because the narrator is plainspoken or the plot needs to be straightforward at that moment, then that is the appropriate way of showing, as well as telling, the story in that line. Sometimes the Voice of the song calls for short, simple words as opposed to flowing, metaphoric, polysyllabic ones.

I could write a line describing a person's journey down the Byzantine avenues of doubt and decision, questioning how history will gauge his exertions. Or I could write, as Bob Dylan did, "How many roads must a man walk down, before you can call him a man?" Is Dylan's line "telling" or "showing," and does it matter when the Voice of "Blowing in the Wind" communicates with such a powerful, plainspoken urgency?

HOW LONG IS THE ROPE?

My college theater adviser, Tony Connor, read a scene study I had written. He looked up and said, "I see this character is at the end of her rope. I'd like to know how long the rope had been." My character was exasperated and emotionally spent. She had no energy, and neither did my scene. Tony correctly identified that the energy of the story would be in showing how she got to where she was.

I've expanded his rope metaphor to include any story that would benefit from more context or prestory. Sometimes our songs can go further and expand their meanings when we have more of a lifeline leading up to the moment at hand.

George came to a circle with a song that named and described different medical procedures (MRI, colonoscopy, and so forth). It went into enough detail to be humorously uncomfortable. The choruses were the reminder that all these procedures are worth it when we get the results. As a listener, Sarah said she wanted to hear more about why the narrator was willing to undergo these tests. We had all gravitated to a short mention of doing these things for his loved ones. We agreed that if the narrator told us more about the life that brought him into the doctor's office to begin with, we would feel more invested in hearing these medical descriptions. It was a funny song, but not a light one. Hearing more about how better health meant time with friends and family would be helpful and appropriate, even with the emotional buoyancy of the narrative.

I realized I needed to show more of the "rope" when it came to writing about the Greek god Hephaestus (god of blacksmiths), forging delicate objects as a way to gently coax his wife, the goddess Aphrodite, to love him. He describes the things he makes with loving detail, "Silver webs with sanded grain / That catch and hold real drops of rain." He says his wife is "more beautiful than when she left the night before," hinting at the fact that he knows she's been sleeping with someone else.

So . . . maybe he's okay with making her beautiful things and sending her off to sleep with another man. Maybe the song is just a nice description of the end of a rope. But we know that can't be true. To give the story the power it deserves, we'll want to know more about the personal tensions he's carrying.

Since Hephaestus is also the god of volcanoes, a volcano metaphor gave me the opportunity to show more of that rope.

Hephaestus says, in the bridge,

> When I'm feeling vexed I go outside and bury something
>   deep,
> Then stand back and push a button, from a distance watch
>   the earth explode . . .

The narrator starts with the word "vexed," as if to say the deep disappointment of his life is merely annoying. But then we get a sense of the deeper struggle. He likes to blow things up and watch the dirt fly up in the air. And perhaps he wants to Blow It All Up, not just the earth, but also Earth. The violence of the daily volcano eruptions in his yard suggests the longer history of pent-up rage at his betrayal.

This Greek god finds peace in his workshop, in creating things, and in being on planet Earth with humans who "wake to know the fire again," that is, who shoulder the humiliations of life and still find ways to create. We know his inner turmoil from seeing the explosive outlet of his rage at being tested again and again.

If our songs have rich descriptions but little movement, points of context can show the friction, the conflict, and the emotional stakes that will engage and invest our listeners more fully. Whether we call it the road of life, the bomb fuse, or the rope, we can look along the timeline for context or pretext that adds the right amount of drama.

DO I NEED A BRIDGE?

I was writing a song with some fifth graders, and Sam asked, "Oh! What about that thing in a song where it gets like this," he bowed his head and frowned, "and it's quiet and serious?" The other kids nodded. They knew that part of the song. I said, "I think you mean a bridge." Yes, that's what he meant. I said I didn't think we needed one. We were saying what we wanted to say without it. The kids agreed.

Bridges step a little (or a lot) outside of the song's picture to offer a certain kind of information. We call these song components "bridges," but I think of equally descriptive words like "perch" or "vantage point" when I create a bridge, because the bridge in a song often feels like it's zooming up to a higher place. Bridges will offer a different mood or even a different narrator, thus giving us more context. But they don't have to hang omnisciently above the scene. They might simply summarize the underlying theme or lesson of the song, thus zooming out to see more of the big picture.

In going through my songs, I saw that bridges often gave me a sense of the "why" of a song. They also came in when a narrator realized that things are a little worse, better, more important, or just different than they (and the listeners) might have thought at the beginning of the song. For instance:

In an easygoing love song, the bridge can say that "I feel like I can't live without you."

In a pleasant friendship song, the bridge might reveal that "this friendship is smothering me."

My narrator might be searching for meaning in her life, but the bridge captures her revelation that "there was always meaning in my life."

Depending on the narrator and Voice of the song, all of the information in those bridge examples can be shared within verses, choruses, and tags. If we feel like we've already woven a bigger picture into our existing verses and choruses, there's a good chance that a bridge would overstate the point.

In a lullaby, for instance, I'll wish for a baby to have a peaceful evening (small picture), then in the next verse I'll wish that the angels will watch over her (bigger picture), and in the last verse I'll wish for her to have a beautiful and blessed life in general (biggest picture). And then maybe there's a little tag that says, "But for now, I'll pull the blanket up around you." Back to the small picture, the little detail that brings us back to the present. Done.

The big picture rolls out in the verses. Sure, we can add a bridge, bringing in another perspective or setting, like "The world can be frightening, but I'll keep you safe" or "We all grow up," but a narrative with no bridge is probably more in the Voice of the song's gentle witness and of the lullaby genre in general.

Usually, my song will nudge me and say, "In order to be the song I want to be, I want to present this extra bit of information that stands apart from the flow of things"—hence, a bridge (or a perch or a vantage point). If it doesn't nudge me, I'm happy to leave the bridge out.

TIME-LAPSE MEANINGS

In these relatively short creations called songs, thanks to unique devices like the repetition of lyrics and music, we can have whole couplets and choruses with second meanings or narrative roles that reveal themselves over time. I call·these time-lapse meanings. A second meaning often emerges in a way that enhances and illuminates the first.

In my early twenties, I worked as an assistant stage manager at the Opera Company of Boston, and whenever we mounted a production of *Madame Butterfly*, I heard how the "ancestor chorus," sung in the first act by Madame Butterfly's extended family to celebrate her wedding, became the melodic underpinning of Madame Butterfly's abandonment in the final act. Madame Butterfly mourns the loss personally, while the ghostlike offstage repetition of the "ancestor" voices adds an extra layer of deep social humiliation.

When I wasn't at the opera house, I was playing at open mics and seeing how repetition and variation, when mixed with the addition of new information over time, could deepen and transform a three-minute song as well as any three-act opera could.

Singer-songwriter Bill Morrissey was a master of time-lapse meanings.

In "The Driver's Song," Bill's narrator is driving peacefully through the night "onto the back roads." He loves "the feeling of this brand-new truck of mine." He enjoys this time when everyone is asleep, noting, "Everybody goes to sleep so early up here."

Then in the middle of the song, the narrator stops his truck, saying,

> I open the side valve,
> Then climb back to the cab,
> And I drive these woods till that big tank empties out.

Johnny Cunningham's violin solo follows as we spend a couple of measures pondering the fact that this solitude "in the darkness of the new moon" is also a perfect cover for illegally dumping toxic waste.

The narrator returns to repeat "I love these back roads" and "Everyone goes to sleep so early up here." Back roads help you keep your secret. Early bedtimes mean fewer witnesses to a crime.

Time-lapse meanings are more than just clever. They underscore hidden themes and present us with complicated characters and truths. They can also be uncanny: something is the same as it was, yet unsettlingly different at the same time. Bill's stories, often set in northern New England, have troubled characters who deal with a darkness and cold that exist inside and outside of their psyches. The narrators find peace and dignity (and employment) wherever they can. "The Driver's Song" doesn't leave us saying, "Oh, I thought it was about *this*, but now I see it's about *that*." The song is about *this* AND *that*. It's about a man who feels at peace, with his new truck, his new job, and time to himself, *and* he's a criminal. Perhaps the peace he feels is not only in the tranquility of the late night, but also in the peace he's made with his compromised ethical choice.

WORDS

WONDERFUL, WONDERFUL WORDS

We have a dazzling range of word choices to support the overall form and message of the song.

As we find words that are appropriate for our narrators and stories, it's just as important to know in general that there are *so many words*. A precise, beautiful, and interesting word can wake up a whole stanza or even a song.

Every time I'm haunted by heartbreak, I hear Bob Dylan singing, "Like a *corkscrew* to my heart" from the song "You're a Big Girl Now." "Corkscrew." What a word.

We can use the beauty of words to beautify the song. I collect words that I love, like "balcony," "thief," "ponderous," "fog," "sleet," "sinuous," "cartographer." When I was writing the song "Emerald," assigning a jewel-toned beauty to the landscape, I wanted a word that described the Columbia River at twilight. Amethyst was the right beautiful, saturated color, and it had a lovely, gentle sound. Did the word "amethystine" exist, longer and more flowing than "amethyst"? It turned out the word existed, but only rarely, and usually in association with a kind of purplish rattlesnake. Perhaps, if people were acquainted with this rattler, they'd have a suggested reference to the snakelike movements of a river. Perfect! I used it.

Words can also communicate meanings in their rhythms, like the comfortingly familiar freight-train feel in Ferron's line "Love don't clickety-clack down a railroad track, it come together and it come apart," from "Ain't Life a Brook."

Verbs are words and worlds in motion and therefore have the power to move us and our songs in stirring ways. When I was developing an image of a pilot taking me to distant, exotic "Mandalay," in the song "I Never Knew," I could say the pilot "took" me there or even "flew" me there, but I went with, "Love was like a pilot, sped me through the clouds to Mandalay . . ." I loved the old-movie feel of the word "sped," and this revved-up verb helped to suggest both the narrator's exhilaration and a lack of control, both of which were important to her experience. One little word can really speed us along.

Just remembering that we have a range of language opportunities can be freeing and expanding. We've come to a place where the Voice has given us the general color and sound palette, the feel, the environment. Now we can go into that song world and find the smorgasbord of words that enhance the mood, focus the narration, and keep the listener engaged with all the pops of vibrant, well-chosen words.

THE RHYME, THE REASON, AND THE RELATIONSHIP BETWEEN THEM

I like to put an alphabet at the top of a work in progress and go through the whole alphabet to try on rhymes to the lines I've come up with. Every word will have its own associations, and sometimes those associations will influence, or even change, the course or the feeling of the song.

One retreater had a song with a line that ended in the word "fashion." The rhyme that went with it was "passion." "Passion" can be a heavy word, but it worked. And I think it gave this young writer's song more teeth. I'm glad he tried it on and used a word that I couldn't imagine him choosing out of thin air.

When I was writing the song "Iowa," I had the line,

Way back where I come from, we never mean to bother, we don't like to make our passions other people's concern.

I went through the alphabet to find a rhyme for the word "concern." My internal dialogue went as follows:

I could go with the word "learn," as in, "I'll never learn" or "I
    hope to learn," but that sounds a little stiff.
"Earn" could be used as "bravery I'll have to earn." More epic
    sounding than I want.
"Discern" . . . is too clinical.
"Turn" is a really helpful word with many meanings . . . but not
    here.
"Burn": Maybe . . .

*So we walk in the world of safe people, and at night we walk
    into our houses and burn.*

That was the line. The word "burn" increased the drama and di-
rected my mind to the contrast between a public and private self. The
more serene you are in the outside world, the more you totally lose it
and burn when you finally get inside. "Burn" felt real to the narrator.
At night we walk into our houses and burn.

A lot of rhymes will disqualify themselves. We tried to rhyme
"danger" at a teen workshop and discussed our options:

"Manger": a little drinking trough for animals that we associate
    with the birth of Jesus. Okay . . . go ahead, try it on (I put it in
    a song once). No? Okay. Didn't think so.
"Stranger"? Maybe.
"Ranger"? Something we associate with scouts on horseback.
    Hmm. No.
We were really pleased with ourselves when we came up with
    "estrange her," and it fit.

There are also consonant clusters and multisyllabic words that
can rhyme. When I had insomnia as a child, I made a game where

I'd come up with an ending like "-air/-ere" and find all the rhymes for it in the alphabet. Nonrhyming words were a negative point (like the nonword "yair") and clustered-lettered or multisyllabic words like "flair" or "ensnare" were a point. If I got to zero points, I won! It was a useful game for a future songwriter.

Finding rhymes is like a jigsaw puzzle. It's wonderful when we find the puzzle piece that fits in the way we expected it to fit.

But the twist is that there will be rhymes that open up meaningful *new* avenues that can influence the direction of a song. Instead of making the rhyme fit with our first jigsaw puzzle, we find ourselves adapting the original puzzle to the new piece! When I found the word "burn" in "Iowa," the narration in general became more sweeping and poetic. The picture shifted, and I liked the new picture better.

However, sometimes in our enthusiasm to finish a song or to not throw away a brilliant line (that unfortunately ends in the word "orange,"), we'll convince ourselves that something fits, even if it doesn't.

So, there's the challenge: by all means, we should let interesting rhymes live for a second or two and decide if they are urging us to adapt our narrative in a meaningful way, but we can't let the rhymes bully us!

Here's a word that bullied me: "sleazy." In the song "As Cool as I Am," the narrator is leaving a romantic partner. For a long time, the line went, "Whoa-oh-whoa-oh-whoa and that's not easy. I don't know why you had to get so low-down and sleazy."

My manager, Charlie Hunter, said, "Sleazy? That can't be the word you want." It wasn't. It went too far. The narrator has some compassion for her ex-partner. She doesn't want to insult him. She just wants out. And "sleazy" is kind of a sleazy word. "But," I explained tersely, "it's almost done, and there is no alternative." Charlie was adamant, and I knew he was right.

The whole song wanted to be done, but I went back to that line, and back, and back.

And there it was:

> *Whoa-oh-whoa-oh-whoa—and that's not easy. I don't know what you saw, I want somebody who sees me.*

That's the summary of the song. It's true to the narrator. It's one of the song's most meaningful lines. It was worth the wait.

LEAVING THE SONG
TO FIND THE SONG

When I was writing "Circle of Love" with Gary Burr, our struggle to find a rhyme wasn't yielding new and interesting directions. With every rhyme we explored, we felt like we were getting further off the path. Here's a good trick for figuring out if our rhymes are helping or hindering the message of our songs. Gary asked, "What would we want to say if we weren't trying to rhyme?" Sometimes we can avoid the wrong rhyme by remembering what we want to say directly.

We talked through the plot and themes that we liked in our emerging song, and our discussion got us back on track with some new lines and rhymes.

Working and reworking a rhyme to be consistent and accurate is draining, especially when there's no guarantee that the perfect line is waiting for us. We are nobly creating something out of nothing, and it's hard to hold the faith that "something" is there. And sometimes it's not. And sometimes we lose perspective. Jumping outside the rhymes for a minute gave me and Gary an escape hatch when we were stuck. Once we were clear about what we wanted, we had more discernment about the couplets we'd begun, and more options for new lines we could invent.

THE WEIGHT OF WORDS

It's amazing how light words often sound light, words like "feathery," "frivolous," "puffy," "wispy."

And then there are heavier words, like "ponderous," "murky," "leaden," "grave."

Literally using light and heavy words can add leavening or gravity to a song. One word can go a long way.

There are other kinds of weighty words, too, ones that have a certain amount of emotional or cultural heft.

Swear words are really heavy, like the word "f*ck." How do you know when to drop the F-bomb without annihilating all the words around it? I have never written a song that can bear the "weight" of it.

Here are some other words that can weigh heavily in a song:

- An act of violence or violation, like "murder" or "assault."
- Intense emotional words, like "detest" or "agonize."
- Cultural taboos or bigoted words, like "slut," "whore," or any number of ethnic slurs. Sometimes we want a narrator who uses words that we the songwriters wouldn't use. This is touchy territory: Has our song earned enough of the listeners' trust for that verboten word or expression to be our best choice?

Once we think about words having different weights, we can use them liberally or sparingly. We can even apply our own subjectivity to how we weigh our words. I think purple is heavier than yellow and that a sin is heavier than a crime.

We can also use words that are heavier than their surroundings and draw attention accordingly.

Lisa came to our retreat with a song called "Chasing Daylight." It was hard to tell if the mention of doctors in the first verse was metaphoric. The chorus could apply to many crossroads:

> It's not a matter of time
> Not a matter of miles
> There's always a perfect rhyme or reason . . .

Then Lisa introduced a heavyweight word in the second verse:

> . . . No prescription,
> No incision,
> I am everything that I need.

Incision?!

It seemed too personal and too specific to be a metaphor; she had raised the stakes with this word that was heavier than its abstract surroundings. "Incision" suggested life and death and things we alter that we can't change back.

We listeners experienced an immediacy like that vertiginous moment when we hear that we should undergo an operation. Lisa confirmed that she wrote this song after a medical recommendation.

Despite its weight, the word "incision" didn't drag down the rest of the song. The effect was quite the opposite. Lisa just knew when it was time to present the real and heavy stakes without losing the sense of hope and transcendence in the overall song.

The Voice and our narrators can lead us to words that are appropriately heavier and more emphatic than the rest of the song. I was writing about the eruption of Mount Vesuvius in Pompeii as a parallel to my own sense of loss. I remembered the suddenness, the way the ordinary day got cut off, midmotion, and the way that every darkening sky now felt like a bad omen.

In the final verse, I also recognized how, connecting the volcano's eruption and my breakup, everything turned to "ashes and dust." That seemed a little vague. It seemed like a good time to diverge from the metaphor of Pompeii and touch on the modern, mechanistic, humiliating aftermath of my experience. The nuance of my pain was that "the trust turned into ashes and to lawyers and to dust." I stepped outside the metaphor as if to say, "Time to ditch the togas and mosaics. This happened now." I wanted that kind of heavy word.

WORDS THAT SHIMMER WITH ASSOCIATIONS

Words like "galleon," whether it's an old ship or an old coin, can suggest an entire historical setting, and phrases like "nip-and-tuck" can hold collective cultural associations.

Just as we know that words have different weights that we can intentionally place throughout our songs, we can use words with strong associations to fill out a story we have only a few minutes to tell.

I made many historical references in "Empire," a cautionary song about fascism and imperialism that I wrote in 2004. I relied on vivid historical flash points to carry their own weight in the course of the narration.

"Get back on your horses and join my next campaign" was a general reference to religious crusades, while the word "campaign" suggested both political and military forays. "The sun never sets on my dungeons or my army" came from the century-long slogan that "The sun never sets on the British Empire." There's a ruler who says, "Kiss my ring," going back to the time when rulers (who were sometimes also popes) held a godlike power over the people.

In a new song, "Let the Wind Blow," I was looking for words that could generally evoke the early-twentieth-century era of bold expeditions, so the protagonists "scaled a deep crevasse." "Crevasse" is more a word from old stories of derring-do than from modern adventures. The narrator and her companion "blazed" through the forest with "machetes lifted high," and, later, she wrote the tale of their adventures with a "golden pen." These are words that refer back to a different age of exploration and even a different era of storytelling.

Considering that words have their own ripple effect of cultural memory and association, if you call a modern bartender a "barkeep," a listener's mind might quickly divert to a burly man serving pints of ale under a whale-oil lamp. So be careful with your barkeeps, barmaids, wenches, swains, grogs, meads, and straw pallets unless that's where you want our minds to go!

GATHERING UP HISTORICALLY AND CULTURALLY SPECIFIC LANGUAGE

Not only can we find words with a shimmer or rippling effect, but we can also look into the word world surrounding our chosen song terrain. For instance, if there is an operating room in a song, we can learn the names of the machines, instruments, special lighting, and staff positions in an ER. Besides scalpels, there are Kelly forceps and retractors. The lighting can be surgery lights, diagnostic lights, task lights, and exam lights. As for the staff, there are surgeons, scrub nurses, circulating nurses, and anesthesiologists (seven syllables, unfortunately) who might be in attendance.

When I was writing the song "We Learned the Sea," I knew I was dealing with a foggy seascape and that I was creating a reflective moment where a sea-captain narrator would be gathering strength before a great challenge.

I got a sense of the era and historical genre that I could work with. I was in a preindustrial "maritime" time. I imagined a clipper ship, a captain who steered by the stars, and also some kind of assistant. The captain speaks of a "first ensign." I could have used a simpler name, like "shipmate" or "young sailor." But "ensign," especially a "first ensign," was more specific, more resonant, and more like a yarn than a story. I used the word "tempest" instead of "storm"; I used the geographically specific term "strait" instead of "place." A captain would make geological distinctions. All of these words conjured, for me, a time before radars, GPS, and motors, where ships were guided by sailing skills, faith, and intuition. I learned some maritime and ship terms that I didn't use, but it was nice to have them available.

Words with heavily laden historical or cultural references are waiting for us once we've decided where our songs take place. We might not use every flywheel, clove-hitch knot, or Parrott rifle we discover when we look into times and places, but it's helpful to gather up words and expressions and see where they can hold layered meanings within the short time we have for our songs.

ADD SOME COLOR

We can literally add some color to make our songs more colorful. When I first wrote about feeling a poetic connection with Canadians in "O Canada Girls," the last verse took place at a fluorescent-lit airport gate where everyone looked a little jaundiced and sleepy. The lyrics presented an image of people who are exhausted by their travels but don't really know where they're going (I created the image to contrast a mythical Canada in the rest of the song). Within this airport image, I diligently started to find rhymes for words like "sallow" and "vacant." I was saying what I wanted to say, yet the song itself seemed to fizzle.

Then I realized that the image itself was flat and lackluster. Was there another way to frame this journey? I went back to the questions of "Where did I go?" and "What happened?" and remembered driving up to Quebec, where the lines and colors of the landscape seemed so bright and crisp. No matter that some of the land was in Vermont! I remembered the view of beautiful lakes and the moment when I stepped out of the car into the bracing air. There was focus and momentum. And there was color.

> If I drove up eighty-seven
> Up past Montreal

Following the bluest veins
Following through icy rains
Would I emerge in the present
And know just where to begin?

I had traveled into a color palette of blue lakes, silver frost, wet brown bark, and glittering green pine needles. These were the kinds of colors I could use to lift the song, and its narration, to a more invigorating, vivid space.

ADD SOME FUN

When Peter Mulvey played his song "On the Eve of the Inauguration," he said he put in a reference to a baby just because it was fun.

> *And I smile in the way*
> *That we hominids do*
> *When we see a little baby hominid*
> *Like you*
> *And you smile back with a look*
> *Of joy or indigestion*
> *And I shiver*
> *Right down to my bones*

There was a lot of weight in this song about politics and our country. The baby anecdote was a welcome addition. Metaphors and vignettes, like single words, can have their varying weights and values. On reflection, Peter pointed out that, simply, "If you want fun in your songs, put fun things in them."

WE ARE THE GODS OF TIME AND SPACE

Does a lyric line have too many or too few syllables? I have some good news. We are the deities who create and control the time and space of our songs: we can make it fit.

Unless . . . it really doesn't fit. Most songs are a mix of massaging the form to fit the words we want to use and dutifully following the rules that the form dictates to us.

When we hear the overall song, we can listen for where we can phrase things smoothly, making our words and melody work together.

If the Voice of a song is one of military precision, with exact rhythms and line lengths, then we must serve that precision.

If it's a haiku, with prescribed numbers of syllables, we must serve that precision.

However, there are many ways to adapt a line to keep the words we want to use. Sometimes this is called "tracking," and other times it's called "phrasing." One retreater explained, before starting his song, that he had not yet "lain" the words over the music. He knew he could stretch, pause, or rhythmically manipulate words to create the emphasis he wanted. We can often finesse a line to use the word "lavender" when we really don't want to settle for the word "purple."

Here are some ways to discern between a creatively manipulated line that works and one that doesn't.

1. It's got to *sound* like it's on purpose. If the words at the beginning of a line sound bunched up, like we couldn't bear to leave out a syllable, our listeners will hear it (and we will, too). If the Voice of the song determines that the narration has a soothing flow, the bunching up of words will be even more obvious and unfortunate.

2. If our listeners can't make out the words because we're rushing through them, odds are that the narration would benefit from better phrasing. Lyrics don't have to be crystal clear on the first listen, but I've often found myself asking songwriters to *help* me hear and appreciate what they're saying. I recently insisted that Jay and Sarah, who were cowriting a song, extend the phrase "The light pours in." I said I didn't want to be a taskmaster, but I really wanted to hear that light pouring in!

3. If we're creating a great, but not easily accessible, metaphor, we don't want to bury it in the song. If someone writes, "She wrote masterpieces timed to cicada invasions," which would be a funny and poignant reference to someone creating art every seventeen years (the amount of time between mass cicada insect emergences), my ear and my mind will want to have clarity and a certain expanse of time to take in the image and the idea. It's often when we get excited about a metaphor that we do our best to shoehorn fourteen syllables into an eight-syllable line, but those are the very same metaphors our listeners will need some time to process.

But even when we're writing something that goes at a very precise clip, we have phrasing options:

We can turn a phrase into a whole line. One retreat songwriter, Kara, had a verse about the Daughters of the American Confederacy. The name got shortened to "the Confederacy." The song's theme, however, had to do, specifically, with white women's actions in history, which made the mention of "Daughters" essential, but Kara couldn't find enough space for those thirteen syllables!

We figured out that Kara could devote an entire line to the name. We found a line that could be taken out and replaced with the long title of the organization, creating the space and accuracy that were right for the song.

Here are some other ways to smooth out our phrasing:

- Often we can take out pronouns at the beginning of a line. "She said she thought she could step away " can go all the way down to "Thought she could step away."
- We can lengthen the time of a word, and sometimes shorten it, or give it more syllables, either to pick up the slack, timewise, or to give something more emphasis. Instead of saying we're angry, we can put in a diphthong and say we're ah-ing-gry.
- We can fit three syllables into a one quarter note with a triplet (rhythmically sounds like trip-a-let). That's how we turn "purple" light into "lavender" light.
- We can lengthen a line or add a whole extra line (I guess you'd call that a tag) at the end of a stanza or verse. The stanza ends "That's where you will find me / Where I always want to be." And we can just repeat the melody of the last line and tag on the line we wanted, "A fish at the bottom of the sea."
- Silence is an excellent ally to words (see below with the song "Empty Plane"). If we add a line or half measure of lyrical silence, we won't lose the listener. The music is still going.

It's also important to put the emphasis on the right syllable in each word. When we force the word "TAILpipe" to sound like "tailPIPE," we aren't sounding like the gods of time and space. An exception to correct emphasis would be a song with a specifically chosen rough-hewn feel or whose narrator pronounces words incorrectly.

One way to make sure things are phrasing correctly is to speak the lines to make sure the emotional and syllabic emphasis is right for the narrative.

If the Voice of the song is conversational and contemplative, there can be more latitude of line length. Sometimes the lyrics can flow as loosely and asymmetrically as a blob in a lava lamp. But it's still got to be a graceful blob. The blob still has to make sense to itself.

Here's how I played with words and silence, paying attention to the overall emotional tenor of the phrasing, in these lines from the song "Empty Plane":

> I leave for a living,
> It's what we all do.
> And I say that I'm missing the ones that I'm leaving,
> And I always do.

Notice how the third line is much longer than the other ones? I did it because I am the god of time and space in my own songs. Symmetrically, this should be a four-line stanza. But technically, I made it five lines, because I could.

I'll put the lines into the four beats of a measure:

1.	2.	3.	4.
Beat	Beat	I leave for a	living.
Beat	Beat	It's what	we all do.
Beat	Beat	Beat	Beat
And I say that I'm	missing the	ones that I'm	lea-ving
Beat.	Beat.	And I	always do.

We can communicate what we're saying and thinking in the rhythm of the delivery. Songs present a theatrical version of these human conversational rhythms and thought patterns.

The song "Empty Plane" exists in a space-filled dreamtime, proceeding at the pace of a bemused narrator encountering a dreamscape. The phrases reflect the psyche of the narrator. She blurts out, "And I say that I'm missing the ones that I'm leaving." Then, perhaps, she thinks that it sounds like she doesn't *actually* miss anyone, and so she adds, after a few beats, "And I always do." The silences also "speak" by filling in the thinking time.

NONVERBAL WORDS

I first heard the expression "nonverbal words" from Steve Earle. I'd never thought of the "oh oh oh" and the "ah ah ah" as words before, but his definition was accurate. These utterances are words that hold the musical space differently than either words or musical passages with no human voice. These nonverbal words communicate something, even if they're saying, "And there's nothing more to say." And not only that, but different sounds also mean different things. "Whoa-oh-whoa-oh" says something different than "deedle-ee-dee."

It's worth trying on a few nonverbal sounds to see what fits the song. For instance, to me, "ah" is gauzier and more contemplative than "oh," which seems to punctuate a thought.

Another function of nonverbal words is to give the listener a sense that a human is still there, adding some emotional companionship. Mark and Jim (who cowrote their first song at a retreat and now perform as a duo) repeat the melody of the chorus "All that's broken is not lost" with "mmm-mmm-mmm." The nonverbal words extend their message by showing they are still with us, unobtrusively humming, while giving us meditative space to take in their verbal words.

If words fail us, as it were, the Voice of the song might be calling for these nonverbal feeling words. We can try on a short one or a string of them, and then intuit, listening to the Voice and message of our songs, whether we want an "mmm-mmm-mmm" or a "doo-be-doo-be-doo."

THAT OLD CLICHÉ

We only have so many syllables in a song. "The Star-Spangled Banner" has fewer than one hundred of them. If we use a cliché like "hot as the sun," we might be giving up the space we'd use for something more illuminating or meaningful to the song.

But clichés can be utilized in ways that are strong and helpful. There are pros and cons.

Also, there's a difference between a commonly used phrase like "warm-hearted" or "cold-blooded" and a "violets are blue" phrase that doesn't say anything at all, and even suggests that the writer skipped the work of "Where did I go, what happened, and how did it feel?"

We get to decide why we're including often-used phrases or even flat-out clichés. Worrying about clichés can bring a voice into our heads that's like a bad, controlling friend. "Pouring rain? That's cliché." "You said, 'I love you forever'? That's *so* cliché . . ."

If you've been working on a song and you realize that you want to be with your beloved "tonight, in the pale moonlight," I might say, "Hmm. Pale moonlight is used a lot. Is that what really happened? Is the moonlight really pale?"

You say, "Yes, pale."

I say, "Maybe take out 'pale,' just to be general, but not sound a little . . . cliché?"

You say, "No, I want an adjective, and I want to use 'pale.' Pale is where I went."

I'll make suggestions: "April moonlight? Spring moonlight? Late? Early?"

If you're not as stuck on "pale moonlight" as the hypothetical songwriter above, you can get away with a cliché and even give new life to it by adding one small word that personalizes your narrator's experience and removes doubt about the lyric's authenticity. Even if our songwriter goes with "pale spring moonlight," they'll establish that they were really "there." Someone can make a reference to the expression "the streets are paved with gold," but say "the freeways are paved with gold." By changing "streets" to "freeways," the narrator accomplishes two things. One is that we believe, by adding this variation, she has really gone there, as it were. The other is that she adds the historical "streets paved with gold" allusions (boomtowns and utopian dreams) of this phrase to her song.

Sometimes we use trite phrases, but we accompany them with beautiful and interesting melodies. If I'm writing a song called "I Love You in the Pale Moonlight" with a riveting melody, I may discover that I'm perfectly happy with commonly used phrases as the vehicle of statements communicated by the music itself. Sir Paul McCartney, of the Beatles, wrote the hit "Silly Love Songs" to show the power of often-used expressions when the music is beautifully developed and when the sentiments are truly felt.

We can also use a cliché to add a little space around an unusual phrase. I used the expression "from sea to shining sea" in the love song "I Have Been Around the World," which I wrote with Rob Hyman, because I'd already said some heavy stuff, especially for the kind of song it was. For instance, I said, "And it's truer now than it's ever been: I'm the lucky one that love has taken in." Love itself is a home that the narrator finds. That's an unusual angle to introduce in a love song, so I was okay with the phrase "sea to shining sea," not to mention "You're all the world to me," because I liked the balance between unusual perspectives and the universal, plainspoken "love song" feel that I wanted to keep.

HARVESTING METAPHORS

When we give ourselves time to explore a setting and we start to develop the metaphors for our songs, those metaphors can come back to reward us later on. We can speak in the language of the metaphor we've taken the time to establish.

This is a verse from "End of the Summer." My room in Hadley, Massachusetts, where I wrote the song, looked out over the fields of two farms, and I could see more farms in the distance. The seasons' transitions were visually defined from crop to crop: asparagus to strawberries to corn to pumpkins to stubbly, fallow fields. One of my verses puts a young girl in this actual landscape as a metaphor for the seasons of her relationship:

> I feel like the neighbor's girl, who will never be the same,
> She walked alone all spring; she had a boyfriend when the
>   summer came,
> And he gave her flowers in a lightning storm,
> They disappeared at night in green fields of silver corn,
> And sometime in July she just forgot that he was leaving,
> So, when the fields were dying, she held on to his sleeves . . .
> And she doesn't want to let go, because she won't know
>   what she's up against,

The classrooms and the smart girls,
It's the end of the summer, it's the end of the summer,
When you hang your flowers up to dry.

I could have ended the verse with, "When you just can't say goodbye" or "When you have to say goodbye." But I looked at the landscape itself and found that I could "harvest" an image from the metaphor landscape, and I wrote, "When you hang your flowers up to dry." This helped me align the feelings, the landscape, and, even better, the turning of the seasons that affects both the feelings and the landscape. There are no more roses and peonies in September. When our narrator wants to remember something, she can dry flowers as a keepsake, and that will have to suffice as her memory of the living, rain-drenched, fragrant bouquet of flowers given to her from a first love.

TRANSMUTATION

There's a moment where not only do we employ a metaphor, but the metaphor is interchangeable with the thing it represents, because the metaphor describes how we experience the magic of something. What does this mean? Example:

One retreater wrote a song in which a child daydreams about traveling as she plays with paper planes. In a later verse she flies to the West Coast. She says she's flying in a "paper plane." By overlaying the child's paper plane over the actual adult experience of flying, she transmutes the magic-infused child's perception with that of a traveling adult.

We all have transmuted ordinary objects into what they magically represent for us. There can be a table from a domineering parent's house taking up all the space in their grown child's first apartment. Poetic transmutation is when the young woman moves to another apartment at the end of the song and decides to leave the table behind and says it can "mutter over someone else's tomato sauce from a jar."

Transmutation is a harvesting of metaphors where the metaphor itself becomes as real as what it represents.

MUSIC
(IN OTHER WORDS...)

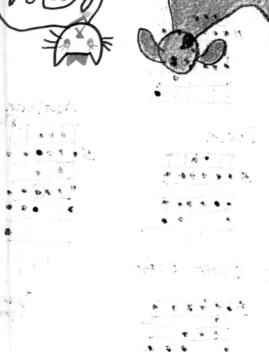

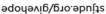

A Mixolydian

0

A Dorian

5

A Blues scale

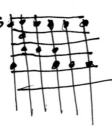

5

Mixo Dorian Bl...

5

Open...
for...

WONDERFUL, WONDERFUL CHORDS

The chords we choose for our songs are constructing musical narratives that ideally support the lyrical narratives, and vice versa. How can we learn about all of those chords out there and get excited about their wonderful role in our songs?

My fellow retreat leader Rick Gedney presented the best way of looking at chords that I have encountered so far. I never learned about music theory because I just learned the chords from where I put my fingers. There are some basic hand shapes that we can make, taking them all the way up the fretboard of a guitar (with or without using the index finger as a "barre" that covers all the strings in a "barre chord"). I memorized the hand shapes and what they were called. Then I learned the other chords in each key (the keys being the "houses" the chords live in). Then I just messed around a bit with altering those chords.

Hence, I have a true theory expert at my retreats. I am not an expert.

Each day Rick would give a "sonic prompt," an interesting chord that people could try out, just like a lyric prompt.

One year the first musical prompt was actually a single note. We talked about songs that drone on one note or one chord, resonantly, hypnotically, or spiritually—a gong, a chant, or an "om" in meditation. That was day one. The next day he played a dyad.

A DYAD MADE WITH THE FIFTH

The next day, Rick presented two-notes, a dyad, with a "one" (root) note and its "fifth," the note that's seven semitones up from that first note on a scale. He plucked them at the same time. The fifth is a harmony note. In my head, the jump between the one note and the fifth, and the sound they make together, always reminds me of the wicked witch's army singing "oh-ee-oh" in *The Wizard of Oz*. That harmony has a very interesting sound, one that will bring up its own individual associations.

THE TRIAD: MAKING A HAPPY OR A SAD SANDWICH

The third day, Rick showed us a "triad," meaning a three-note chord, where we put a note between the original note (it's our anchor note, so we call it the "1" or "the root") and the "fifth" he had shown us the day before. He showed the two ways a chord could go, traditionally, in becoming a three-note chord, or a triad. If we go up three semitones on a scale from that original note, we'll get a minor chord (called a minor third), and that chord will have its associated feelings. If we go up four semitones on a scale, we'll get a major chord (called a major third). Likewise, we'll have certain feelings that we associate with a major triad.

In about three minutes, Rick had shown us how to make a traditional chord. It's a little tricky to count the notes in a scale. Why? Because in the scale of notes, some notes don't have a half tone between them. To do a counting of steps, or tones, we have to know where the semitones are. We showed this in the "Chord Houses" chapter, and we'll show it again. The whole scale looks like this (the "#" means sharp, which means a little *higher*; an A# is a half step *higher* than an A):

C	C#	D	D#	E	F	F#	G	G#	A	A#	B
1	2	3	4	5	6	7	8	9	10	11	12

Notice that there is no sharp note between the B and the C, and the E and the F!

When most musicians collaborate in the studio or in rehearsal, they speak more in "flats" (meaning a little *lower*, represented by a "b") than in "sharps," so this is the same scale in flats:

C	Db	D	Eb	E	F	Gb	G	Ab	A	Bb	B
1	2	3	4	5	6	7	8	9	10	11	12

Again there is no half step between the B and the C, nor is there one between the E and F. That's just the way the cookie crumbles! Keeping this handy chart nearby, here's a way to think of how we can build the chords we'll use in songs. To make a triad (I call it a chord, but there are many chords, not all of them triads), pretend that the "1" (the original note) and the "5" (the note that's 7 semitones up) are two pieces of bread. Then make a "happy" sandwich with a "3rd" (the note that's 4 semitones up) in the middle, or a "sad" sandwich with a "minor 3rd" (the note that's 3 semitones up) in the middle.

To me, the main triads, major and minor, are like the known sandwiches of Western civilization: bacon, lettuce, and tomato; peanut butter and jelly; egg salad and watercress; and the like. But we all know that chords, and sandwiches, can be so much more complicated than that. So, let's see what Rick did on days four and five to these major and minor triads and think about how many interesting sandwiches there are out there, even if some of us are more than happy to stick with a BLT or PB&J.

OTHER TRIAD CHORDS

After Rick Gedney introduced the best-known triads to us, the major and minor triads, what I call the happy and sad sandwiches, he showed us other triads. He varied the triad by replacing the "fifth" note, which is technically one of the pieces of bread in our triad sandwich, by *augmenting*, going up, or *diminishing*, going down, by one semitone. Then he showed us how we could make a "suspended" triad by raising the "third" (the filling of the sandwich) by a semitone (or lowering it by two semitones).

FOUR-NOTE CHORDS

There's a "chord" with two notes (whether it's technically a chord is up for debate) called a dyad and a three-note chord called a triad. What is a four-note chord called? It's called a four-note chord. When we explore four-note chords, the skies open and a huge range of possibilities comes pouring down. The one that I will describe is called the "seventh" chord, because it shows up most often in even rudimentary folk songs. I'll illustrate with a D chord. A D chord is made up of these notes: D, **F#**, and A. The Dm chord is: D, **F**, and A. But we can also change a finger placement and go two half steps (frets, piano keys) down from the D note to a C note and get a D7 chord: **C**, F#, A. We can keep the D in the chord, too, played on a different string or piano key. So there we go: a seventh chord is a four-note chord that adds a note that is two semitones down from the "root" note.

VOICINGS

Different voicings of chords happen when we play them in new configurations. I can play an F chord with the F note in the middle of the strings. Or I can anchor an F chord with a barre (using a finger to cover all six strings) where the F note is deeper and lower. Sometimes I alternate between these voicings in the same song. One F sounds lighter, while the lower barred one gives me more gravitas.

We can make different voicings of a chord all the way up and down a fretboard or keyboard, and they will all have their own moods.

Another interesting thing that will happen as we experiment with chords in different voicings is that they will often add that fourth or fifth note that alters the original three notes (triad) of the chord, and we can decide if that extra note is helpful or unhelpful to our narration.

WONDERFUL, WONDERFUL CHORDS, ACHIEVED BY KNOWING SOME MUSIC THEORY OR JUST MESSING AROUND WITH MUSICAL IDEAS!

Every chord we make will have a name. We don't have to know the names, but imagine how interesting it was to discover, at fifteen, that I had made a Cmaj7 (C major seventh), when all I knew was that I had replicated "the chord that sounded like Joni Mitchell's 'Chelsea Morning.'" Whenever I wanted that Chelsea-morning mood, I knew I could henceforth play a major seventh chord.

Knowing the names of chords is important when we're making music with other people in a band or in a studio. It's also helpful for knowing the "moods" of the chords, so that we can use them again, and for transposition, or changing the key of a song.

What I formally know comes from about ten years, on and off, of guitar lessons. Most of my discoveries, however, have been very freelance and self-taught or friend-taught. I love exchanging chord ideas with friends. If I make a C chord on my guitar and slide the whole thing up two frets, I make a D chord . . . well, sort of a D. This cool C-chord shape that I play two frets up will add an E and a G to the D chord and remove the A. Rick would call this an "Em9 or Daad9/11/E." I call it "misty" (I'm not sure what kind of sandwich it would be . . . whitefish on a bagel?).

This is a book about writing a song that matters to you. There are a million charts that show you how to make the different chords, and you can even find this information for free online. I'm hoping to show that we can make these chords both by trial and error and by learning them (with or without charts) from friends and teachers.

Remember, Rick showed us chords that were just one or two semi-tones away from one another. That means that by sliding a finger a little this way or that, we can listen for the sounds we want. Much of my life's work comes from sliding a finger this way and that.

I'll start with a chord, the members of its chord house (or key), and all their moods (major, minor, and so on). If I want some extra lift or tension, I can visit a neighbor's house and borrow a chord.

Sometimes I'll create the same chord shapes going up the guitar neck (or keyboard) to see what interesting variations (or "voicings") I can come up with.

But most of the time I'll add a finger or remove a finger from a chord and see what happens. In my mind I associate these chord vari-etals with pictures, words, or moods.

One time I started alternating between two variations on an Em chord. I didn't know what they were called. But they sounded disso-nant, a little metallic, and monochromatic. The repetition reminded me of a life-support monitor. That chord progression became the ba-sis of "Mortal City," the long song based on the true story my house-mate had told me about the voluntary blackout during Philly's ice storm in 1993, during which everyone turned off their power to help the hospitals keep running.

Those chords are called A#dim11/B (A sharp diminished 11 over B) and Gm7/B (G major seventh over B). But I knew them as a heart monitor in a hospital during an ice storm in "Mortal City."

MUSIC THEORY AND WRITING SONGS

KJ Denhert, who teaches at our retreat, moves adventurously up and down the fretboard of her guitar in every composition. The prosody—how lyrics and music support one another—in her songs, and even her covers, is a joy to experience.

The song "Esmerelda," for instance, has cadences of Flamenco music to suggest the strength, beauty, and passion of an old college friend. Her cover of the Beatles' song "Help" is slow, moody, and complicated. When she sings, "Help me if you can, I'm feeling down," we really feel the deeper sadness of that request.

We were having a group discussion about the merits of knowing music theory, considering that there is a whole school of musicians who suggest (never overtly) that no one has the right to write songs or music without a solid theory foundation.

KJ turned theory orthodoxy on its head when she said, casually, "Oh, I know all that stuff. I just don't use it when I'm writing songs."

THE WEIGHT OF NOTES AND CHORDS

Just as words have different weights, the dyads, triads, diminishments, and sevenths can add and subtract narrative weight as well. The lower frequency of an open E note on the guitar (as low as you can go in standard tuning) can add emotional gravity. When I was writing about how artists have to live with less payment (or no payment) for their work, I sang, cheerfully, the line "Oh, you're gonna give it all away." It's a breezy progression of major chords starting with a G. At the end of the song, I gave the message a little gravity. I found that starting with an Em chord, with that lower note ringing out, saying, "You're going to give it all away," underscored the narrator's empathy for artists who (understandably) have a hard time with this message.

There are high notes that we can add to major and minor chords to remove some weight as well. Or we can go to a higher chord.

While Rob Hyman and I were working on "This Is How I'll Free Myself," narrated by a person who finds what he calls freedom in drinking alcohol, we were letting the low-register minor (sad) chords communicate a deeper story. The narrator knows he's not kidding anyone about losing his time and life to drinking. So, we wrote the lines "We shook the last drops from Glen Garioch's finest hour. We sipped them like the blood of Burns." (Glen Garioch is one of the oldest Scottish distilleries, and Burns refers to the Scottish poet Robert Burns). We ended these lines with an appropriately somber A minor chord. Or so I thought.

Rob raised his eyebrow, looked at me, and played a D seventh (D7) chord on his keyboard at the end of the line, which was higher, lighter, and from a completely different chord house. Borrowing a playful seventh chord from the house of D was the equivalent of inviting a friendly, childlike voice to a sad, grown-up house.

I soon realized the D7 was crucial to the song. Even though the narrator's subtext is one of sadness and loss, he is still speaking with hope. There are *many* alcohol-based bonding experiences, the narrator could say, such as when we reverently savor every drop of a classic Scotch whiskey with poetry-loving kindred spirits . . . right? The higher, lighter D7 holds the narrator's question and faith. Maybe all this drinking has replaced a meaningful life, or *maybe* it helps to *create* a meaningful life . . . right?

The higher chord added to the emotional range of the narrator and the song.

Knowing that chords and notes have different weights, we can add their lightness and heaviness to a song's communication of "what really happened."

The wisdom that life is often "tragicomic," where there is something sad in every happy experience and something happy in every sad one, can express itself in the poetic wisdom of different chords and musical juxtapositions. Likewise, there is impermanence in all reality, meaning that we might put a dreamy major seventh chord in a song about building a cabin, and there are things we can point to and call them real, continuous, and reliable in the midst of imper-manence, planting a major chord in a dream sequence about floating furniture.

The different valences of our musical choices can reveal the dap-pled light of emotional ambiguity or the ambiguity of reality itself.

ANOTHER THING
ABOUT CHORDS

Every chord can communicate a different mood, color, and transition. They are all wonderful in their own ways.

No one chord is better than the others.

Except the B7. It's amazing.

CREATING A BRIDGE
(WITH LYRICS) MUSICALLY

We can do a range of things to set a bridge apart from the other parts of the song. Here's my cheat sheet.

We can do the following:

1. Start the bridge with a chord that's a housemate in our key, not the one we started with in our verses. For instance, if I'm starting a song on a G chord, and my song is in the key (or house) of G, the two other chords (housemates) in that key are C and D. By going to a related chord, I am saying, musically, "This point is *related*, but different."

2. Go to a whole other key. The point we want to make with a bridge will determine if we want to stray off the path and go to a whole different key, or house. One caution: we'll probably want to get back to our original key, and we'll have to find the right-sounding musical path to it!

3. Stay with the same chord that began the verse or chorus but use a different/varied melody.

4. Start with the minor or seventh version of any chord in the key of the song. Minor and seventh chords can often connote reflective moods of memory, hope, and melancholy in our stories,

so in a bridge, with its reflective vantage point, we might find these moody chords establishing a sense of perspective and "what I learned from reflecting on this" in the narration.

5. Go to a different voicing of any chord in the key we're playing.

6. I've noticed that sometimes I take the melody of the second half of the verse, called the pre-chorus, and see if it will work as a bridge melody with the change of a note or two.

Wow, a lot of options! I think a lot of people just go with number one.

WHICH BRIDGE
TO CHOOSE

A song's Voice can guide us on how to proceed musically in a bridge.

When I was writing the song "Emerald," my narrator was searching for some cohesive thread in the eclectic travels of her life. After two verses, I heard a harmony that I could sing with the verse, and I recorded it so I could sing with it. I realized that the harmony, with higher notes than the verse, had its own melody and could be a bridge! Sure enough, a higher melody with the verse's chords matched the narrator's "higher" vantage point, which in this case is the wisdom of the future self:

> Unbeknownst to my pride, I had filled my memories
> With these hours of gold and emerald light.
> I can plunge my hands into all this time I've lived,
> And the jewels run through my fingers.

Another song, "Let the Wind Blow," has two verses that describe the narrator's swashbuckling adventures. The bridge plays on the cinematic feel of the narrator's journey, so a key change felt like a good, dramatic choice, sticking with a sense of excitement while also announcing that this information is coming from a new perspective:

As we scaled the deep crevasse,
how we marveled at our fortunes
and the genius of our ways . . .

When I was writing from the perspective of a five-year-old in "The Babysitter's Here," the narrator underscored the fan worship of her babysitter with a bridge about a family outing to see her dance recital. This important new information about seeing her babysitter as a Dancer on the Stage was easily communicated by *gently* rolling to a different chord in the same key:

And we all went to see her go dance at the high school,
We made her a big card,
And she told us that she'd be the unicorn
Wearing a pink leotard . . .

For each of these songs, the different function of the bridges dictated whether my shift would be higher, lower, subtle, or dramatic.

BUILDING A
MUSICAL BRIDGE

A musical bridge, or instrumental bridge, has no words or it has non-verbal words. How we arrive at a musical bridge, musically, is similar to our musical approach to a lyrical bridge. The Voice of the song can guide musical bridge choices just as much as lyrical ones.

In "The Ocean," my "sea shanty gone awry," the musical bridge drones on and on, like ghost sailors bleakly waving their beer steins in the air. In "Summer Child," Rob Hyman's rolling triplet notes race like bicycle wheels.

Musical bridges are a time both to digest the lyrics preceding them and to communicate feelings that are ineffable, meaning unable to be expressed in words.

In terms of instrumentation (instrument choices) for musical bridges, we might hear instruments as we are writing a song. From the start, I heard horns in the song "You Give It All Away."

I've also enjoyed letting other people come to me with their own ideas, once we're in the studio. I'll describe feelings, pictures, and even colors, letting other musicians step out and interpret what I'm saying, so the decision about how to proceed becomes a dialogue.

LITTLE BITS OF MELODY

As our songs take shape and we find the melodies and rhythms that interest us, musical fragments and freestanding musical lines might pop up here and there. We walk around the world with a melody, and these associative music lines spin off from them.

Value these offspinnings! I've learned to hold on to fascinating musical mutations. They become instrumental hooks, narrative bridges, instrumental bridges, variations on melody lines, descants, and unusual taglines.

When I went into the studio with some impressive studio musicians in 1995, I played Steve Miller, my wonderful producer, "The Ocean." I mentioned, almost with embarrassment, that I had a nonverbal melody line to add. I remember saying, "It just seems important . . . " Steve made that melody line into an eight-measure instrumental/nonverbal word bridge, and it also became the music that the song went out on, also called "the outro," or "outro music." "The Ocean" is heavy in lyrics and ideas. This added-in melodic "la la la" countermelody was the perfect aeration for the density of the narrative.

I heard an eerie little four-measure melody that fit with the song "Empty Plane." I grabbed my phone and recorded the melody (along with some chordal ideas to capture the ambiance). It was such a joy to hear Trevor Gordon Hall replicate this unique musical passage, which added some valuable, spooky contemplation time between the verses.

This is all to say, keep those related strands of melody! When we're further along in the writing of a song, we'll often recognize where they complement the existing parts of the song and add valuable emotional and musical variations. And, if they have nothing to add to this song, perhaps they can provide a springboard for the next.

CROSSROADS AND ENDINGS

THE BEGINNING OF THE END

So here we are: we know where we went. We know what really happened and how it really felt. We found the Voice of the song and metaphors that worked in the song's world. We also found the chords that tell the musical story. Oh, and one more thing: we like the song!

Looking over the song when "the ink is *not* dry," when it's not all the way finished, can actually be the most exciting part.

This can also be a point of evaluation where we have our moments of unexpectedly severe doubt. We might imagine our listening friends' faces going cold or even looking a little embarrassed for us.

We think we might want to share the song with the world, but we realize, hopefully without panicking, that part of it doesn't feel quite right. "I just want to fight you / I love you to fright you." That sounds weird, and it doesn't feel true. Now that I've read through the whole song, hearing and listening, I take a walk, run through those lyrics, and think about what really happened and how it really felt: "I don't want to fight you / I love you despite you." *That* works better (or does it? I take the time to keep finessing if I need to . . .).

We might find ourselves feeling calm and methodical, zeroing in on the small change of a single chord or the removal of a half chorus to replace with nonverbal la-dee-dahs. Lo and behold, with that minor amendment, we go from liking the song to actually wanting to play it for our friends.

We're in the harbor. The song is a song. We still may have dramatic moments and negative feelings, and we will often have at least a few last decisions to make, but we're making changes within a song that has a known structure and a distinct Voice. The finishing time can be a reward.

MAKE IT MAKE SENSE
FOR THE WRITER

If a song makes sense to us, that doesn't mean that we have to understand every line that we wrote perfectly. I remember writing the line "And that's when you knew this world can't be saved, only discovered," thinking that I *almost* knew what the line meant.

One of my narrators, sad about the dizzying speed of the Information Age, called the internet "the silver hope kaleidoscope." Without putting my finger on why, I knew my narrator had summed up a downside of on-demand enlightenment and entertainment.

I have definitely written songs with lines that hold some latitude of mystery, even for me. But sometimes we find ourselves with a collection of beautiful images and chord progressions that, like the Pied Piper, lead us nowhere. What does this song mean? I'm not asking this question on behalf of the listener. Songwriters have to check in and make sure the song makes sense to *themselves*.

People with very beautiful voices can be the most self-deceiving. At one retreat, Joseph wrote a song that had bears from different fairy tales throughout the verses. The images were provocative, but they didn't present a through line or have a common denominator. I asked Joseph, point-blank, "Do you understand this song?" Joseph said no.

"Aha!" I cried. "You have a beautiful voice and a song with interesting words and images. We will follow you on the journey of this song. We will trust you. And if *you* don't know what it means, you're basically leading us into the woods." I added, "And not the good kind of woods."

The good kind of woods leaves us exploring and making connections. The bad kind of woods just leaves us feeling lost and even a little left behind.

Joseph agreed and figured out what aspects of bears in fairy tales were interesting, important, and thematically unified for the song. On the other side of this exploration was a wonderful, provocative song that made sense to all of us.

We create characters that become strong enough to speak for themselves, sometimes with their own cryptic interior logic, but we are doing ourselves and the world a favor by coming to a personal understanding of what our narrators say, no matter how inscrutably they deliver their stories.

LEAVING THINGS OUT ON PURPOSE: THE INVISIBLE B

There's a reason to leave things out in a way that might confuse some people. The people who can relate to what we're saying will feel all the more connection when we *don't* spell everything out. A true kindred feeling doesn't require abundant explanation.

My most successful songs have been ones that don't necessarily have universal appeal (although they all connected with more people than I expected).

I call this omission of certain explanations the "A, B, C with an Invisible B." The listeners who can relate to the narrator's experience won't need, or even want, all the information.

There was the line from "After All": "When I chose to live, there was no joy, it's just a line I crossed."

A. I chose to live.
B. (unmentioned in the song) When I emerged from a clinical depression, there was a time when I was healthy enough to show up for therapy and go to class. It was an intellectual limbo period, where, yes, I was in the clear for staying alive, but things still felt vague and unhappy.
C. There was no joy, it's just a line I crossed.

I knew that I was giving enough information to the people who had been through a depression like this and probably not enough information for people who hadn't. I knew that fellow sufferers would recognize this crucial yet unceremonious line between death and life. The song is not a primer for people who have never experienced depression with suicidal ideation. It's for those of us who have made a certain climb up from a certain kind of rock bottom.

WINKING

What is winking? It's putting an inside reference in your song. I've done it. I referred to friends who

> give me purple flowers and orange tea,
> On goose-down spilling quilts and turquoise chairs.

That was a nod to my friend Kate's apartment. Winking was okay in this song, I believed, because the image also fit the song. There was a universality to the easy, colorful friendliness of the image and the friendship it represented.

But then there was a song by a college student at a workshop . . .

He said something about "Always wearing that blue sweater."

My associative mind wondered "Which blue sweater? Is that a metaphor, perhaps for depression? 'Wearing the blues?' It's itchy, hot, and burdensome?" My mind filled the gap as I tried to understand. And then I thought, "Or it's just a blue sweater. Not everything is a symbol!"

But then there was the next line, "Yeah your cat enjoys the weather."

"Cat? Who and what is this cat?"

I cried uncle. "You've got a lovely voice," I said at the end, "but I'm lost."

The boy smiled mischievously and said, "Yeah, there are a lot of things that only my friends would get."

He wasn't creating universal (or "Invisible B") metaphors; he was winking to his friends.

We can write songs for our friends, but trying to follow a song I could never understand just gave me a headache.

THE SONGWRITING STRIKE ZONE

How do we know if we're presenting the "Invisible B" in a song or just making a reference that no one will get? How do we know if we're only winking to a small group of friends? The answer is that we guess. In baseball a pitch to the batter can go too high, too low, too wide, or too inside for a perfect connection with the bat. The "strike zone," a box of space between the batter's heart and knees and as wide as home plate, provides the best opportunity for the batter to hit the ball.

What a great analogy for the purpose of our songwriting! The potentially home-run-hitting connection exists when our songs reach the audience's core, somewhere from the heart to the knees. When the song is very general, perhaps it's too low to make a connection. When a metaphor is very complicated, it might be too high. Too personally close or inscrutably far away from our listener's home plate, their known terrain, will also be less ideal for them to connect with what we are pitching.

However, there's still a lot of space in that strike zone of collective experience and emotional honesty, and often when we're presenting a poetic reality that has been truly felt and honestly observed, we're taking a courageous chance that our words and music can lead to a very rewarding THWACK of recognition and connection.

THE SENTIMENTIMETER

Does your song sound too mushy to you? Does it sound so sentimental that you don't want to finish it or perform it?

I hope you won't abandon a sentimental song if it feels true to you and you secretly like it that way.

However, we have another option when we encounter what feels like too much sweetness. We can run our songs through the Sentimentimeter, the internal measure of sentimentality, and determine where we'd like to firm up any unwanted softness.

I was walking around New York City, working on the song "New York Is a Harbor" that I cowrote with jazz musician Bryn Roberts. The descriptions throughout the song showed how, historically, the harbor-like embrace of New York City allowed diverse groups of people to make a living and forge a unique kind of history.

I came up with a bridge:

> *We cheer for the Hard Luck Joe on payday,*
> *The dancing girl when she gets to Broadway,*
> *The workers' lunch on a crossbeam in the sky.*
> *So don't you let yourself forget.*

Logically, since I was making an emotional appeal to remember what we "cheer" for, I could have ended the bridge with, "So don't you let your *heart* forget." But I preferred the word "self."

That was the Sentimentimeter at work, drying up the lines of the song that felt a little too damp or gushy. The truth was that I was appealing to the whole listener, the one who felt with a heart, thought with a mind, and walked with feet that knew hard city sidewalks.

The word "self" was a matter of accuracy, and a part of that accuracy was presenting a love of New York that was more than just sentimentality.

A certain amount of dryness also allows the listeners to feel their own feelings as opposed to being guided to what they are supposed to feel.

"The One Who Knows" has a pretty sentimental chorus, sung from a caregiver to a child:

> *You'll fly away, but take my hand until that day,*
> *So when they ask how far love goes,*
> *When my job's done, you'll be the one who knows.*

The word "job" is casual, conversational. It rhymes with "slob" and "blob." And it's there for a reason. The narrator could say, "When day is done, you'll be the one," or "My labor's done, you'll be the one," or something a little more epic than the word "job" suggests. But I wanted the everyday closeness of the conversation between the narrator and a child. I also wanted to take the emphasis off my emotions at that moment. The song was more about the universality of letting go than my personal feelings of loss. I didn't want to prescribe a feeling to my listeners through the register of an ode or an elegy.

CLEVERNESS

I wrote the song "Buzzer" with a narrator who feels cornered and rushed. She is not clever, at least not in this song. She speaks quickly. She talks about "they" without explaining who they are. She jumps from topic to topic. Now she's in a Chinese restaurant. Now she's driving to the university. Now she's trying to navigate a science experiment she's a part of. She speaks in verses that rhyme, but not very well, and not all the time. She doesn't speak cleverly.

Likewise, the chords in "Buzzer" suggest some emotional complexity in the way that they bounce around between major and minor triads, but they are basic chords that don't have any ambiguity.

Perfect rhymes are clever. Interesting chords that suggest nuanced emotions can be very clever, in the way they present both a narrative complexity as well as a musical virtuosity. The Voice of the song might not prove to be so clever. We might love something very twisty, smartly rhymed, or musically complicated in our songs, yet still feel like there's something a little wrong. Certain genres speak broadly to "folks," in a straightforward way. Certain narrators feel clumsy or unsure of themselves. In the case of "Buzzer," cleverness might have suggested more emotional containment or control over the situation than the narrator had.

Tracie came to a retreat with a song in which body parts such as her head, her hands, and her feet "speak" to her about how to get through the grieving process. But later she mentions what the books are telling her and what her friends tell her. Tracie stepped outside of the clever device of body-part metaphors, because the song was an honest and creative exploration of grieving, not a cleverly impressive catalog of all the different ways her body spoke to her. The unexpected addition of metaphors outside of the body register gave her song the humanity and warmth of a weary narrator whose heart is on the mend, not the songsmithing cleverness of metaphoric connections with the head, hands, kneecaps, and gallbladder.

THE TWENTY-YEAR RULE

This is controversial. I counsel against songs that have things in them that were introduced to us in the past twenty years. A song that is *specifically about* a new smartphone app or store that's opened in the recent past is an exception. So is a snappy, funny song.

My fellow songwriters are always trying to figure out why I have this particular aversion when usually I'm pretty open about whatever a person puts in a song. Here are my thoughts:

1. References to the far past, like daguerreotypes, steamboats, and the Rockefellers, have accumulated meanings. They have become touchstones and metaphors. Modern references (from the past twenty years) can resemble news and current events as opposed to images that connect to tacitly universal themes.

2. It takes some time to discover the value of certain events. Historically, some things that once towered in significance hardly get a footnote, while other historical events were well known but came into more focus over time. I know that the uprising at Stonewall Inn in New York City was a pivotal event. Pet rocks from the seventies didn't have any historical staying power. Even now, you might ask, "What the hell is a pet rock?" My point exactly.

3. There is often a feel of time in songs that is not historically fixed. For instance, if I say, "You called me," that's different from, "You called me on your iPhone 10." Unless there's a specific reference that we're making, the time and brand location can be distracting. An intentional reference could be, "You always had to be / Better than me then / I got an iPhone 9. / You raved about your iPhone 10." That said, in five years, we'll be on to iPhone 30s, so the reference to an iPhone 10 might be more quaint than we intended.

I put the word "Starbucks" in a song. The song took place at an airport, where there are always Starbucks coffee shops. Starbucks put the accent on the right syllable (I couldn't make the word "café" work). As an institution, Starbucks has been around for more than twenty years. Still, I wondered, does this emphasis on the brand sound more like a trend than a known collective symbol?

In one song circle at our retreat, Ellie made a reference to Twitter with a line about a woman who's "afraid to rock the Twitter feed."

To humor me (and my thing about twenty years), the group played with other words. A line about "the Feed" replaced the reference to Twitter, and to me the replacement sounded more to the point, thematically. The Feed implies a mass-media appetite with no beginning or end. When we "feed" something that's formless but that still has a life of its own, this faceless entity aptly defines itself as the Feed.

I thought it was a great change. In the end, Ellie used the words "Twitter feed," because Ellie knows my recommendations are not sacrosanct, to me or anyone else!

IT CAN MEAN FIVE THINGS

For those who believe that the listener determines the meaning of a song and that the meaning is all up for grabs, I say . . . not for me, as a writer or a listener. If we truly believe a song can mean anything at all, we can spare the songwriter some time and direct the listeners to a dishwasher manual.

But clearly songs are special if (because?) they can apply to a range of the listeners' realities. So, I relent. A song can mean more than one thing. It can mean five things.

At some point, the Voice of the song, and its metaphors, will have an internal logic, and that cohesion will limit the scope of interpretation. Suzanne Vega's song "Blood Makes Noise" came into my head when I was waiting for some medical test results. I wondered, had Suzanne written the song in the voice of a person at a doctor's appointment, about to hear some important test results?

The narrator is addressing a doctor in the song. Check.

The narrator's blood is pumping so fast, she can hear it. Check. I could hear my blood, too.

The narrator is speaking quickly, as if she doesn't really want to know what the doctor is going to say. Check.

Suzanne herself later said that she was creating a moment out of context, not wanting to commit to "one set of circumstances." But still, this wasn't just a song about being deeply anxious about *any-thing*, like the prom or a basketball game. The anxious narration, the questions to the doctor, the riveting expression "Blood makes noise," and even the mechanical sounds in the production show us that the stakes are high, and they tilt toward a visit to a medical professional or some kind of scientific expert.

There was not one line in Suzanne's song that was out of sync with my interpretation of a patient waiting for medical results. In fact, I felt like Suzanne was employing the "Invisible B": she was creating a strong kindred bond with those of us nervously sitting in the doctor's office without explicitly confirming the setting. Maybe my interpretation wasn't exactly what was in Suzanne's mind as she wrote it, but I can't imagine ten wide-ranging scenarios where the lyrics and music would have been a perfect fit, and I was grateful for how the chosen environment spoke to my general situation, regardless of what remained pretty widely open to interpretation.

For us writers, we want to make sure the song can mean a limited number of things to *us*. When the voice in our heads says, "This could mean twenty things, and that's cool," perhaps, instead, this is a moment to focus and check in with where we really went, what really happened, and how we really felt. When we are aware of the core of our experiences, we can still decide to give it a narrative that suggests many meanings.

I think my friend Tamar Avishai, host of *The Lonely Palette* podcast, summarized it well in an interview when someone was asking if postmodern art could have a specific meaning, given its abstraction. Tamar cited the "It can mean five things" position I had taken.

"I think what Dar meant is that a piece of work can mean a lot of things . . . but it can't mean *anything*."

GO NO FURTHER!

An almost finished, or relatively pieced-together, song can still hit some emotional danger zones as it nears completion.

There is a point in the journey of many songs when a craggy sign appears out of nowhere. It says, "GO NO FURTHER!" It may have a crudely drawn skull and crossbones or a prone stick figure with two X's for the eyes. These symbols of foreboding will probably have a strangely childlike visual register.

Should we heed the GO NO FURTHER! sign? No. We may choose to stop writing a song. I've put songs away before. I haven't found an interesting-enough melody, or the concept is so complicated that it can't fit in one song, or maybe I can't find the core of what I wanted to say. That's a bummer.

But the nearly panicked GO NO FURTHER! sign is something different. I encountered it as I cowrote that song with Jill Sobule about the joys of FM radio in the 1970s. I felt the love for the material, I knew the feel of the song, and we had a chorus I liked. I remembered every minute of the afternoon Jill and I had spent going through all the Billboard charts of 1974–1979. I had pieces of two verses, an idea for a bridge, and a chorus to build on, but . . .

The whole song had started in my head with the line "Remember, Bruce Springsteen divorced a model and married a musician." Now

I had a problem. Bruce Springsteen had divorced the model in the 1980s. How could the song still take place in the '70s? Could I go to the future and look back on this time? How could I do that?

An anxious voice started to take over. Suddenly, things went from open-ended and curious to personal and self-incriminating. How *dare* I do that? What started as a question had devolved into a crisis.

The sign loomed up ahead. GO NO FURTHER!

Anxiety became absurdism. In an instant, it just seemed like a terrible idea to finish the song. It was somehow even *offensive*.

I imagined getting a call from Bruce Springsteen telling me to mind my own business.

Then his wife would call and say, "You are callous. These are real lives you're writing about."

Then his ex-wife would call and say, "I'm also an actress, you know."

It's when I imagined the Springsteen pile on that I knew I could and would finish the song. I would never get those phone calls.

Every time we write a song, we are putting something new into the world. We are exposing ourselves. I make a point of telling myself to go ahead and write the song I'm writing and then see where and if it lives in the world. Maybe it has a short life, or maybe it's the surprise hit of the record (often the case). Or, yes, sometimes a song just isn't going anywhere, and there is no further to go, and it doesn't get finished.

But usually the GO NO FURTHER! sign appears, suspended on a rusty chain, just before the Aha! Moment where something clicks and the way is clear. This is to say, GO NO FURTHER! shows up before we are about to have a finished piece of work that exists in the world. You and I, and a whole lot of people we know and don't know, are about to see this Thing We Made. That can be scary.

In "FM Radio," my breakdown moment became a breakthrough. The third verse would take place in the present with a '70s FM-radio acolyte counseling a young music listener. She's telling the younger person to turn up the volume, play a musical instrument, and own her musical experience loudly and proudly. She drives her point home by saying, "Remember, Bruce Springsteen divorced a model and married a musician."

So, when we see that dread-filled sign that suggests that we are inherently incapable or unworthy of writing the song we set out to write, I say, VENTURE FORTH!

THE AHA! MOMENT

And then it happens. We go further than the GO NO FURTHER! sign, and there it is, the Aha! Moment. We're sitting there with a lot of "what" in a song that we're writing. We know *what* the melody is, *what* the basic structure is, and even *what* the Voice and setting of the song are becoming. And then, aha, the *why* of the song becomes clear.

I wrote the last line of "Buzzer" an hour before showtime in New York City. "Buzzer" is about Stanley Milgram's Obedience to Authority experiment of the 1960s that was designed to measure obedience (and was also a study of fascism). Usually, people excoriate the citizens who participated in this experiment and "obeyed" the "authorities" to the point of inhuman cruelty. My song had a different perspective, and therefore I thought I had already found the *why* of my song: I was making a controversial defense of a woman who obeys an "authority" voice and inflicts electric shocks on a stranger (the shocks weren't real). She's not a bad person. She's broke and she's intimidated. Can't we understand her experience with some empathy? I, for one, thought I could.

Arguably, I was defending someone accused of fascism. My defense of the would-be fascist was enough of a *why* to make an interesting song, right?

But as I was putting on my makeup, wanting to perform the song when I went onstage in two hours but with exactly one line missing, I got a very strong feeling as a line came into my head: "When I knew it was wrong, I played it just like a game." This was the Aha! Moment. I always cry when I have it. That's how I know.

Part of me knew I hadn't found the real Aha! until now. There was an extra layer to find. This wasn't just a narrator who woke up and realized she had done the wrong thing yesterday. The Aha! Moment was that *she knew she was doing the wrong thing as she was doing it*, and she had to wake up the next morning with the knowledge that she had *knowingly* participated in something that felt immoral. And she *still* had to live with herself.

I remember the Aha! Moment of every song I've written. The Aha! Moment can be very small, but it is usually a moment of recognition. It's *why* I wrote the song in the first place. And in my experience, it's a moment worth waiting for.

BRINGING US IN FROM THE START

I always love a first line that pulls me in. Once we're up to speed on writing a song, we can revisit the first lines to see if they can engage the listener while remaining consistent with the rest of the song.

Here are some ideas that my friends and I have used:

Asking a question: "Are we the fools for being surprised that a silence could end with no sound?"

Saying something weird or provocative: "I don't go to therapy to find out if I'm a freak."

Engaging curiosity: Two of our retreaters, Chris and Marie-Claude, started a song by repeating "I saw it coming" a few times. I wanted to know what "it" was!

Presenting a colorful or vivid image: "The columbines are coming up down by the gate."

Early in my career, a fellow songwriter explained what needs to happen right up front in a song: The Who. The Where. The What.

I couldn't disagree more. It might serve your song to begin with a precise image, like "In the mist of silent fields on the morn after Antietam . . . ," but, like the opening shot of a movie, there are many angles that initially bring us in. The examples above are soft images or partial images. The song itself brings the initial images into focus. We do not have to have all the information up front.

Why am I talking about the beginning of the song at the finish? I'm hoping that you, the songwriter, can discover a dynamic first line that is organic to the rest of the song. Once we have a sense of our song, we can decide which "establishing" POV (point of view, in film talk) works the best. We can make that decision anytime in the songwriting process, but the start of a song might become more self-evident after we've gone from start to finish.

WHEN WE DISCOVER THAT OUR MELODY IS THE MELODY OF ANOTHER SONG

Sometimes a melody comes into our heads that just feels good and natural. The verse flows into the pre-chorus that flows into the chorus, and it feels magical. It's just meant to be. In the backs of our minds, we wonder if this is the melody of another song, but we dismiss that little voice and continue writing. The song is almost done, and, sad revelation, it is indeed the melody of ABBA's song "Waterloo."

Don't worry! The most important thing is to *catch it*, to know what we've inadvertently copied. Change a note here, change a note there, maybe change a couple of notes per line. We can follow the same internal guide of what sounds pretty, interesting, and consistent with the emerging Voice of the song, and then it's all ours. And no one is the wiser.

THE LITTLEST THINGS

I got to meet Rodney Crowell during the spring that I was finishing up my tenth album. I told him I was going back into the studio just to change a few lines.

I wanted to change a lyric from "brought us to bed by a luminous dawn" to "brought us to bed by *the* luminous dawn." I had realized that *all* dawns are luminous. They are defined by illumination! To say *a* luminous dawn suggested that some dawns are not luminous. So, I had to change the lyric to "*the* luminous dawn."

If I had not changed the lyric, it would always bug me. All I said to Rodney was that I wanted to change the word "a" to "the" and "a few other little things."

Rodney said, "Oh, that is so important." It was affirming to have the writer of such iconic songs respond so earnestly to the fact that I was heading back to a studio that was sixty miles from my house, spending three hours with a producer and engineer, just to make these adjustments.

Some songs are all about a certain feel, and we might want to keep what we have, even if it's loose and lacks a little cohesion. But other things might stick out after a few look-overs and think-overs of our songs. In that case, Rodney Crowell and I both support the serious songwriting business of deciding to change a one-letter word to a three-letter word, and vice versa.

BRINGING OUR SONGS INTO THE WORLD

BRINGING OUR SONGS INTO THE WORLD

We can put our songs into the world in a few ways: finished, unfinished, or as a hybrid of "it might be finished." We can play them for friends, we can perform our songs if we can get a gig, we can be in a formal song circle (of critique and support), or we can go to an open mic, where we perform with the audience's understanding that we're not looking for heavy judgment, but we are curious about how we are communicating. Maybe the song is done? Maybe it's not? No matter how we encounter the world with new music, there are ways to make sure the emphasis is on whatever feedback *we* are looking for, be it clarity, communication, growth as writers, commercial appeal, or even the ability to make people cry (in a good way).

ONE-ON-ONE FEEDBACK—THE PASSENGER SEAT

The song is finished. We've gotten far enough past the crossroads of doubt to have completed a song. Maybe it's our first song; maybe it's a new genre. For me, there's always something new that makes me sit on the edge of my chair when I play it for a first listener.

Here I offer some emphatic advice. If a person doesn't like or doesn't get your song, play it for another person before you give up on it. I was lucky enough to have five or six friends who were first listeners to my songs. They were supportive and intelligent, but inevitably there would be a song that one of them wouldn't understand.

Because I write songs myself, I know how far a little feedback can go. I know that the listener giving feedback can cross a line that sends a person not only shutting down a song, but shutting down the whole pursuit of songwriting. Consequently, there are certain things I try to do when I'm asked to be a first listener.

Likewise, when fellow retreat leader Michele Gedney brought me her song, she knew from our song circles how to establish the best environment so that my listening could be helpful to her.

These are some things we did to make this a positive exchange.

1. She handed me a printout of the lyrics.

2. I pulled out a pen and reminded her that when I mark up a page, I may just be writing thumbs-up signs and smiley faces next to things I like (watching a person make notes while we perform can feel foreboding).

3. She and I both knew that some people prefer not to see the lyrics when they first listen, and some songwriters ask listeners to hear a song without seeing the lyrics. I like to make marks based on first impressions, so I like having the lyrics.

4. Michele told me what she was looking for, specifically. She didn't want to tell me what the song was about because she wanted to know if I could tell. Sometimes she and I play songs for each other and start by saying what we're hoping to communicate. Other times we'll ask, "Do you think this needs a bridge?"

5. She went ahead and sang it! We can take a *long* time to explain things before we start to perform, because we're anxious about the feedback.

6. The first thing I did was to say how much I liked the song (because I did), and then I pointed to one thing I specifically liked. If I hadn't liked the song in general, I'd find a part of it I liked or something that I thought was "working" and start from there. There is an emotional and practical reason to start with what we like. Emotionally, I am affirming that this song has a right to exist and that the songwriter isn't making a fool of herself for playing it.

   Pragmatically, I am putting myself next to her, trying to align my vision with hers as she navigates how to improve the song she wants to write. If Michele had played "Twinkle, twinkle, little star, how I wonder what you are," I would say, "It feels soothing and childlike, perhaps like a song for a child," instead of "That sounds pretty simplistic."

7. I responded to her specific question. I thought it sounded like it was about coming home. Michele said it was a certain kind of home. Did I know what it was? I did not.

8. Michele explained what she was going for. She wrote the song about coming to our songwriting retreat. She was coming home to the meeting rooms, to the river views, and to our community of songwriters. It suddenly seemed completely clear to me! We talked about whether there could be some language to show the specific place she was referring to, or if, conversely, she liked it as a coming-home song that could have a few meanings.

9. I pointed out a few things that I hadn't understood, like did "this" refer to this day, this home, this experience?

10. I *paused* before I made some specific suggestions. It's risky to suggest specific words or ideas, because ideally we want to *help* the songwriter steer. We don't want to take the wheel. For better or worse, I tend to have a lot of ideas, and sometimes I make suggestions of words, repetitions, or phrasings. I qualify my feedback by saying that I'm about to add my own idea to the mix as something to try on, not as a prescription. Often I'll ask if it's okay to do so at all, and the songwriter can say no or "not yet" if they feel like a suggestion would interfere.

I was lucky that one of the first listeners to my first songs was Kate Bennis, now a professional performance and communications coach. I'd tell her that I was writing a song about a pack of vigilante New England mothers, the loneliness of postexpressionist paintings, or teenagers in heaven. Years later, she said she had no idea where I was going with my ideas and half-written songs. She said, "But I trusted that you'd make them work, and you did!" Early on, she committed to starting with encouragement and pointing to what she liked. If she was at a loss, she didn't tell me to give up. She said to keep going.

The best listeners, like Kate, won't be backseat drivers, telling us what we can't do, nor will they grab the wheel and tell us what we should do. They will be next to us, happy to be with us on the ride, unscrewing the water-bottle top for us, excited to help us get to the destination we've chosen, and expecting that they, or someone, will enjoy where we end up.

SONG CIRCLES

A song circle is a place where we show up, sit in a circle, and one by one sing a song, or part of a song, where the "ink is not dry" (the song is not finished). We get feedback from fellow songwriters or just get the experience of a first audience with no feedback.

After an open mic at the Naked City Coffeehouse, someone told me about a jam session/song circle at someone's house. That's how it is in your early twenties. Someone tells you to go to some house, and you go. This was just a one-off song sharing with no feedback except for things like, "Cool. Yeah, hey, that's cool." I loved the songs I heard, I loved the camaraderie, and I was hooked. I wanted to hang out with these Boston folksingers. I wanted to write songs where they'd say, "Cool. Yeah, hey, that's cool."

Since then, I've been part of three song circles. In the first one, I was twenty-three, green, and excited. We were fellow sensitive songwriters, and we spoke to each other as we would want to be spoken to (sensitively). Yes, there were hurt feelings from time to time. There were romantic attractions. There were awkward moments. It was easier to give feedback to some songs than to others. But our Wednesday meetings kept me motivated and connected.

The second song circle, out in western Massachusetts, was even better. My songs were more focused, so the feedback was more specific and helpful. There was a range of attendance from people who were pursuing a career in music to people who just wanted to understand themselves and their songs a little better. This was the song circle in which I wrote the songs for my first CD, *The Honesty Room*.

The songwriting circle I'm in now is the group of friends with whom I run the songwriting retreat. We all make a living, or some of our living, from performing music. We don't meet regularly, but every time we do, we feel more motivated to value the time and focus it takes to write a song. A big part of all these song circles has been encouragement and the goal of having something to play for our next scheduled meeting!

As a rule of thumb, song circles are process oriented. We engage our discernment to help each other say what we want to say as opposed to engaging our judgment to say that something simply works or doesn't work. As writers and listeners, we feel safe to rely on curiosity, open-ended creative inquiry, empathy, and even playfulness to guide a search for clarity and impact. When we are collectively focused on the process of communicating through our songs, there is nothing to prove as songwriters. We are only there to improve our songs.

One thing I've learned from having song circles within my songwriting retreats is that we don't benefit from long critiques. We set a timer for ten minutes of feedback after a person has finished their song. We've already established an ethos of trust that excludes snarkiness or observations about the merits of a song based on its marketability. But even in this supportive environment, our songs can get away from us, sometimes irretrievably, when we spend a long time with other people's impressions of our work in progress. I heard about thirty minutes of feedback once, and it took me a week to get back in my own head and access the original inspiration and Voice of the song.

STARTING A
SONG CIRCLE

Something magic has always happened in the song circles I've joined. When the focus is on the process of creating a song instead of how good the "product" is, we are all on each other's sides, and that spirit shows up in how we respond to songs.

I'd recommend taking a circumspect, grassroots approach to finding or creating a song circle. Open mics are a good place to casually ask if there's already a song circle going somewhere. I wouldn't take it personally if you hear about a song circle that you're not invited to. There are many reasons people keep their song circles exclusive. Sometimes they feel anxious. Sometimes they just want to spare you from Fred, the Twenty-Verse Sea-Shanty writer.

We can start song circles, too. We can literally swap songs with one other person, and then add another person, and then discover we are sitting in a circle formation. Voilà. A song circle.

If the grassroots community isn't connecting you to a song circle, you can put up a sign or post something on social media. It's also remarkably effective to share songs in a live online song circle.

There are ways to communicate and questions to ask that will establish a constructive environment. We can use expressions like these:

- I liked it when you . . .
- I really felt that part where you . . .
- I'm curious about . . .
- If this were my song, I might . . .
- What is the relationship between this part of the song and this other part of the song?

In the best-case scenario, we're telling the truth as we ask these questions. We listen for things we truly like, we take the time to precisely identify where there is confusion, and we are on the same side as the other songwriters, truly hoping to help clean up the confusing or convoluted parts.

There might be a room in a place of worship or a free community space for a song circle, but they're usually at houses. Another thing to do, therefore, is secretly figure out who has the best house for your song circle. In our circle, we love Rick and Michele's house, so the rest of us bring the salads and desserts or just . . . show up.

"I'D LIKE A CLUE"

If you have major structural questions about a song, or it's just not registering, you won't be insulting the writer if you ask for a little help.

At the retreat, we were listening to a song that got confusing. This can be an uncomfortable moment, because, as with some Emily Dickinson poems, sometimes it just takes a few listens for everything to make sense.

Or maybe there's a personal story a limited number of people will understand. As mentioned in the "Invisible B" passage, maybe the writer has left something out on purpose.

But there we were, a few years ago, with the presentation of a confusing song. We scanned the lyrics quietly, muttering things about images and pieces of melody that we liked. And then Mary said, "I'd like . . . a clue."

Everyone seemed to exhale, myself included, when she asked for that. She explained that she thought she knew where we were in the first verse, but then in the second verse she was lost.

Asking for a clue was exactly what we wanted, just a little context of where we were, who we were dealing with, what the conflict was. The writer didn't realize that he'd left out some crucial information. He asked if he added this line, would we be on track? A resounding yes.

A year later, I got to try out Mary's clue question. Alissa brought me a song that seemed to focus on a strange relationship with someone who was narcissistic yet extremely loyal, very present minded and alert but really loving their sleep, and strangely enamored of many different smells. I couldn't get a handle on how these bizarre qualities added up to . . . who was this? A friend? A partner? I gave in. I asked for a clue. The song was about her dog.

It's okay to have a little mystery, to let the song have some growing room in the long-term listening experience. It's another thing to lose your listener because you forgot to add the salient information that helps it all hang together.

In Alissa's case, she was entertaining the idea of letting the subject dawn on the listener, in the same way that Emily Dickenson doesn't come out and say that "A Route of Evanescence" is about a hummingbird. I recommended a little clue in the song, or a challenge to the audience to guess who the song was about. Otherwise, out of the blue, we'd be trying to appreciate a person who seems particularly adorable while physically nudging us, who sleeps belly-up on the couch all the time, and who really loves stew.

OPEN MICS

I was too afraid to play at the first open mic I went to, the Naked City Coffeehouse. My friend Jay Shambroom and I went together. He'd been playing guitar for a year, and he just walked in and wrote his name down on the sign-up sheet (fourteen slots, one song per person). I had been playing guitar for twelve years and writing songs for four years, but I couldn't get up the courage to write my name.

Everyone loved Jay. The next week, I signed up. I could hardly sing or play. But I managed. Chris Dunn, the emcee, gave me a "Yeah, that's cool," nod. I came back the next week. And then I played at a range of open mics over the next two years. I started taking undemanding jobs to pay the rent and taking more time for guitar lessons and songwriting. It was an immersive but inexpensive education. For three dollars a night, including coffee, going to open mics was a challenge to my skills, my nerve, and my ego, and it was cheaper than grad school. I made excellent friends with insightful fellow writers. I learned to respect how people created things, and I tried to find some love for all the things that people created, and there were some very weird things. Finding a way to appreciate other people's works did not dilute any standard of writing for me. Going in and figuring out how people communicated through diverse forms and messages helped me find compassion and respect for myself as a writer. I highly recommend attending a few open mics.

For many people, especially ones whose work and lives depend on known definitions of what is correct and incorrect, open mics take a little getting used to. A man shows up in a business suit, carrying a briefcase, and he looks around as if to say, "What have I gotten myself into? I don't even know where to sit." Nervously, he signs up, gets some decaf, and discreetly removes his tie. And then, at nine thirty, he's up. Someone adjusts the guitar mic for him. He plays a song he's written, one he's never even played for his friends or his ex-girlfriend (a lot of people come to their first open mics after a breakup), and he is amazed to discover an audience that appreciates him. He writes more songs, and he comes back, drinks more decaf, and soon after joins a song circle. He likes being a compatriot of teenage poets, songwriting English teachers, and part-time professional singer-songwriters. A year later, he's a more confident songwriter, and he's also a more confident person. Someone walks into his favorite open mic, a woman in a business suit with a briefcase, and as she heads over to the sign-up sheet, she looks around like she's wondering what she's gotten herself into. He tells her it's worth going to an open mic a few times just to open up our minds and because they can actually be life changing. And a year later, they get married.

STARTING AN OPEN MIC

When I played at open mics around Boston, the Nameless Coffeehouse was in a Unitarian church. The Cantab Lounge was a bar, Johnny D's was a rock club, the New Moon open mic was in a town hall, and the Naked City Coffeehouse was in . . . I don't know what it was. I think it was a common space between some offices. Then it moved to a church. There were also cafés, restaurants, and converted barns.

There are many auxiliary spaces for open mics, but I will always recommend starting one at a high school, if it's open to the community. High school students can test their public personalities, shine in new areas, take chances, and experience the power of art itself. If an administrator says no to it, you can find another administrator. If the whole administration says no, there's always a teacher. I would recommend a science teacher first, believe it or not. Science teachers are a bunch of dreamers—mark my word.

An open mic needs the following:

1. **A sound system.** Your sound system can be small, and the output can be modest. I'm not a sound person, and even I know what an open mic needs in general: speakers, cords, mics, mic stands, and a sound board to plug everything into and mix the

sound (make it louder, softer, more bass, more treble, and what-ever is in between).

2. **Some stage furniture and extra instruments.** Chairs, guitar stands, music stands, and piano benches for the performers are also helpful. If someone donates a conga drum, guitar, or key-board, things can run more smoothly and offer an opportunity for young people, people with broken instruments, and low-income participants to play.

3. **Someone to run the sound system.** Someone will offer to help with this. They just will. We can put it out there (at a lo-cal music store, with a flyer, at another open mic) that we want to start an open mic, or we can watch a video on how to run a sound system ourselves. The better the sound person, the better the night, and it is essential that someone figures out how to eliminate or minimize feedback (electronic noise that comes through the speakers), because shriller frequencies can damage hearing.

4. **Lighting.** Again, nothing fancy. It can be a couple of freestand-ing lights just to direct our attention to the performer. Can we pull off an open mic with just the ambient lighting of lamps? We can try, but this might be the first time some people have performed, and it's nice to give them some flattering, focused lights that are mounted on poles or from a ceiling.

5. **Places to sit.** Chairs, pews, pillows, and a clean floor can work.

6. **A sign-up sheet.** This is literally a piece of paper with num-bered lines for the slots available for the night, plus a waiting list. Or there can be a book of sign-up lists that holds the record of sign-ups over time, like a guest book.

7. **An emcee (or MC, the master of ceremonies).** This is the per-son who introduces each act. This person is a crucial part of the

open mic. Ideally, the emcee will be a low-key, good-natured art lover who gives every performer respect and support. They will have to deal with small crises from time to time, from solving tech problems to buttressing a "limbo mic" where the faulty mic stand makes the mic and the singer sink lower and lower, but mostly the emcee's gifts will be in respecting the new performers, normalizing the weird ones, and harmonizing the whole night.

8. **Bathrooms.**
9. **Water.**
10. **Brownies (for instance).**
11. **Coffee.**
12. **Permission to use the space.**

Things are pretty loose, even at a formal open mic. An informal open mic, like an outdoor one, can function without electricity, but amplification is very useful for soft voices and anxious performers.

Open mics also open up communities. We get to see the mail-delivery guy recite his poetry. We find out that the head librarian was at Woodstock. And we are allowing ourselves and fellow song-writers around us to explore art that is "audience based," which emphasizes how the art moves people, over "commerce based," which places importance on aggregating whatever market statistics and algorithms show what is selling well.

"Commerce-based" music can be just as moving and creative as "audience-based" works, but discovering in real time how we move people, especially people who value the courage and commitment of the creative risks we take, can keep the creative playing field more open.

SONGWRITING RETREATS

I can't decide what's best about songwriting retreats, the mutual support and guidance of retreat leaders and fellow songwriters, the space set aside just for songwriting, or the fact that someone else is doing the cooking. There are retreats led by professional songwriters and teachers, but one could conceivably go to a hotel or friend's guest room and cordon off a given time and space as a retreat. I'm going to describe my Writing a Song that Matters retreat to give a sense of what my friends and I do. Hopefully, this will illuminate what a conventional retreat is like or present components that can be incorporated into a more DIY experience.

A RETREAT DAY

Here is the overall shape of the day.

We start at 8:00 a.m. with yoga, which is entirely optional. Our yoga teacher knows about the themes of the week and likes to weave them into the retreaters' yoga experience.

Breakfast starts at 9:00, and at 9:30 we give the prompts of the day: There will be a "phrase with words" that can have many associations, for example, "And then the wheel turned." Rick Gedney then plays the "sonic prompt," usually a chord. Raquel introduces a color or image of the day. We have weekly themes, like "Chaos into Order" or "Universe into Self" (Monday: cosmos/outer space; Tuesday: society; Wednesday: community/friendship; Thursday: family/friend; Friday: partner/self).

We make it really clear that these prompts and themes are for people who want jump-starts, big and small, into their songwriting. We want to engage the imagination and the realm of poetic reality.

When we meet after breakfast, I deconstruct one of my songs for a half hour or so. Whereas I've used my songs in this book as examples of certain songwriting devices, the song deconstructions will take a single song from where it started to when it was done.

Later, we all meet in a number of small groups and hear songs that people are working on. We usually get to about eight to ten songs per song circle (about ninety minutes). Someone sings a song, and then we turn on the timer for ten minutes of feedback. We offer three song-circle times per day, and writers usually go to one or two of them.

We offer short trips to places that might provide metaphors or even poetic landscapes, like museums, sculpture parks, historic ruins, beaches, and mountaintop vistas.

At night, we turn down the lights, Raquel lights the candles, and people sing their own songs with no feedback (except applause). They sign up ahead of time, which makes it harder for newer songwriters to lose their nerve!

After our song circle, there are late-night snacks in the dining hall. I head off to bed, but most of the others *do not*.

Many people head off to a room where they can continue swapping their own songs. Others love to sing cover songs together. We've tried to create two different spaces, so there's no conflict of interest between originals and "All Billy Joel" or "All Indigo Girls." People stay up later and later, which definitely affects yoga attendance.

MORNING PROCESS

When I started my retreat with a small group, I wanted to offer a range of "creative processes" so people could figure out what worked for them. Here's the sequence I recommended for the mornings that went from around 10:00 a.m. to lunch at 1:00 p.m. I've also included variations to show how people tailored the process for themselves over the years.

1. Personal page: For ten to fifteen minutes, write out a page of whatever is on your mind, perhaps something that feels obstructive or distracting. *But* try to write toward a resolution. For instance: "I feel embarrassed by what I said yesterday" can become a spiral of anxiety that takes up a whole day, so we try to create a temporary solution like, "I can repair this, I can backtrack, or I can let it go. It's okay."

   Variation: We can blow off writing a personal page, write a poem or a poetic-thinking take on something as the "personal page," or write about something that feels like it could become a song. One retreat member said he didn't want to risk getting mired in anxious thoughts; could he skip it? Absolutely. And then I decided to skip it, too!

2. Empty page: For twenty to thirty minutes, with the goal of writing a song, sit with an empty page or a page of lyrics you're working on. This is one of the hardest things to do.

    Variation: A writer can draw a picture. Conversely, if she's on a roll, she can just keep going until she's done, regardless of time!

3. "Take it for a walk" (or just move it around): For forty-five minutes, move around with whatever ideas have come up. Let the wheels continue to turn with some literal, physical movement. There are a lot of paths and passages in and around the places where we hold the retreat. These paths offer many metaphors! There are freight trains, rivers, tall trees, flower gardens, and places that have a little history, like old houses, some old ruins, or a cemetery.

4. Take it to an instrument or a friend: For an hour or so, poke around with an idea. Maybe there's a friend who can sing or play along to help flesh out a song, or this is a time to take up an instrument and try it out (an instrument can be used at any point throughout the morning).

    Variation: One can also be silent or return to the page to write down whatever came up while moving around.

PERFORMING FOR AN AUDIENCE

The words that helped me break through and find my equilibrium as a performer were "You are giving a gift to the audience. You are not asking for something." The relationship went from "Do you like me?" to "This is what I'm offering. I hope you like it." A show that feels dead or badly received can still do a number on me. But performing for an audience of ten people or more is how we can find out how our songs connect with the world, imperfect a science as it is, and sharing our art is part of a bigger personal and overall human experience than we have when we keep our songs to ourselves and our pets.

For most performances, not including open mics, there will be a sound check. A sound check, two to four hours before a performance, is a way to get familiar with the stage. The reason we have sound checks is not just to know how the audiences will hear our performance; it's also how we'll hear ourselves with extra amplification (or in a room with no amplification). The more we know about our stage environment, the fewer surprises we'll have on the stage.

But even with no surprises, putting ourselves onto a stage can challenge those parts of our brains that are experiencing the audience as "them" or The World. What does The World think of this thing that I created? And it's not only the thing itself that we think might be assessed . . . This is, after all, a thing I said "mattered to me." So, on some level I'm asking what "The World" thinks of "Me."

Some people say we should imagine the audience naked, basically limiting the menace of the mob by reminding ourselves that everyone is vulnerable and human. This can be helpful, if a little extreme. When the time comes to perform for an audience, there are many little tricks for keeping our nerves in check, like looking at foreheads, breathing to and from the bottom of our lungs, lowering our shoulders, and thinking our very best friends (or pets) are out there watching.

But there's another energy that one can harness on a stage. What I have also discovered is that once I'm out there, I am a part of something that's bigger than my performance. We are all learning something, and we all want things to go well.

Audiences often can't believe we're being so courageous as to present our poetic realities, our music, and our voices in public. We can actually listen for, and feel, the way that, in live performance, both the performers and the audiences are in this together, hoping to find something uplifting and enlightening. I've even been able to hear the silence between the lines of my songs. I can hear the audience listening. I thought I was alone in this observation until a fellow performer was driving me back to my hotel from a gig in Salt Point, British Columbia. He said he saw me listening to the listening of my performance.

How beautiful that a live performance is such a distinct phenomenon that it has a unique presence. Instead of listening for whether we're doing okay, we can listen for the feeling in the room, the energy of sound and of quiet, and The World that is the community of performer and audience.

There is a valuable education that can come from performing over time. In the short run, every audience will have a person glaring at us or who we think is glaring at us. There will be a squirming child. Some audiences will generally be more rowdy, while others will be more pensive. I played a show for a small audience near Salisbury, England, in 1996. They were so quiet and earnest, I thought they were feeling embarrassed for me. Not so. We spoke after the show. Not embarrassed. Contemplative. Other shows, however, have indeed been gloomy. All of these shows we do as performers, however, will teach us something about our music overall.

There is a myth that we are not and never should be influenced by audience feedback. For the longest time I knew I was influenced by audiences, but I didn't have a name for what that influence was. Peter Mulvey identified what I was experiencing. He said that all the generalized feedback we get, especially after years of performing, can guide our songwriting. Peter said he's noticed a "process of accretion" where having a sense of what will work in his songs "becomes instincts and not analysis." Single members of the audience, such as the bored child, the blind date who hates our genre of music, the drunk woman who loves everything and claps out of rhythm, and the steadfast cousin who comes to every concert, are individuals. But then there is the feel of the audience in general, over time. From my audiences, I've learned how to introduce new material, perform songs, enunciate certain lyrics, and, yes, how to write future songs. We think that audience impressions will limit the scope of how we create, but, actually, it's from audiences that I've learned how to keep writing songs that feel important to me. My audiences have responded more to my closely observed poetic reality than I ever would have predicted. One of the reasons I keep striving to be honest in my songwriting, in fact, is that my audiences hold me to the high standard of honesty.

BUZZ VERSUS HYPE

We may ask ourselves, "Am I writing this song for love or money?" I will submit that when we think poetically, write things that are interesting and beautiful to us, and pay attention to the Voice of our songs, there is already some love in the process of creation. We can write songs for love *and* money.

When something achieves some kind of commercial success in the world, I've seen two ways that people will "commercialize" music. One is by amplifying the buzz, and the other is by creating hype.

Buzz is the natural excitement that occurs around something, like buzzing bees. Buzz is the band selling out local bars in Athens, Georgia, then playing in Atlanta, then Asheville, North Carolina, and finally establishing a circuit of gigs and a community of listeners, regionally and beyond. The music business will expand radio networks, help publicize, and generally point a big sign that says "ISN'T THIS GREAT?" to whatever already exists.

Hype builds on buzz and is sometimes purely manufactured excitement, but usually it's not so cynical. A passionate music fan can show up at her music-company job and say she wants to use all the publicity wheels she can find to promote a band she loves, promoting the band as "essential listening," "the next big thing," or "the band on a standing-room-only tour," neglecting to mention that each venue holds twenty-five people. That's hype. Conversely, someone can look at *PollStar Magazine* and scan the numbers for a band that's selling well, and she can simply do everything possible to *hype* those numbers upward with whatever sleight-of-hand *hyperbole* she can find.

There are a few important things to learn from buzz and hype. One is that there's nothing like the pure buzz success of knowing that every person in the audience has found us, chosen us, and paid money to hear us again. Another is that hype is not necessarily an artificial thing. It can be as simple as a person holding up my publicity photo, where I'm staring pensively on a rock by a stream, showing me five other photos of artists sitting on a rock by a stream, and saying, "How can we make you stand apart a little bit, especially since you don't write songs about rocks and streams?" It can be color-scheme choices, recommendations (and money advances) to go out with better musicians, or an enthusiastic pitch to a radio presenter to play our songs.

Where hype becomes too blown out is when we, as artists, feel like we're being asked to do something that undermines our vision or our values in order to amplify our work, or when we're asked to change the message of our music in order to get more listeners.

A friend signed up with a major label and called me to ask what she should do, because they said they loved her music but that they wanted her to write a pop song that they could bring to radio. She was afraid that she was being asked to do something that was artistically compromising. I asked if she had ever written a sugary, fun pop song that she liked. She said she'd secretly always wanted to write a pop song and that she had some good ideas. Then we talked about all the pop music we love. She stayed with the label. She wrote a pop song that she loved (but that radio stations, alas, did not; not every pop song is popular...).

We get to decide how it feels when the buzz of our work is being spun into hype and whether that hype is pushing us to turn our art into crap that puts commerce over art. It's very personal, and the fear of hype can keep us from growing and learning in the company of great musicians and music-business people.

Then again, it's tough when I hear music on the radio that I know has been designed to be played on a car commercial (a lot of snaps and claps, general lyrics about loving the journey of life, and an instrumental bridge that can be talked over) or an episode from a TV series (snaps, claps, general lyrics about finding my way, and a nice string of nonverbal words). As a person who has worked with many people in the music business, I've always found myself regularly checking in with my folksinging friend Utah Phillips's advice to "make a living, not a killing."

THE SONGWRITER
(YOU AND ME)

THE SONGWRITER

People ask if my songwriting has changed over the past thirty years. I say no, my songs have not changed much. My songwriting process hasn't changed much, either. My experience of myself as a songwriter has definitely changed. I've learned that every song has a moment where I feel like it's "too" something: too long, too short, too personal, too Leonard Cohen or Stevie Wonder (how dare I?). There are more "toos": too predictable, too idiosyncratic, too silly, too serious. I have learned to shrug and say, "Maybe. We'll see," and continue writing.

When a voice comes into my head to say I, as a person, am "too" something to be a songwriter, let alone write good songs, too lazy, too unschooled, too late, too spent, too uptight, or too flaky, I have also adopted the shrug. "Maybe. We'll see."

My practice has become marginally more refined, my diet is marginally less processed, and my writing space is marginally more organized than it used to be, all of which are associated with good habits, but the most important thing that I've improved is my attitude toward myself as an artist. I am committed to believing in myself (and in anyone who wants to write a song).

And I also believe in the power of songs themselves. Sometimes, when that voice is feeling particularly anxious about going further, it even attacks the whole phenomenon of making music.

Fear of change is a powerful force. As we learned when we saw that sign that said "GO NO FURTHER!" the voice of fear will not hesitate to use negative comparisons, self-doubt, self-recrimination, or even an existential questioning of music itself to keep us from shining our light and seeing what happens next.

So, I will finish here with some thoughts that have helped me as a songwriter, in hopes that they mean something to you, a fellow songwriter.

WE ARE ALREADY CREATIVE

Creativity is defined as the ability to find new ideas and solutions. Creativity is not what we create; it's the synaptic transactions that go into the things we create. We might believe that creativity is employed only in making art and that only some people are creative. But if I find a way to turn leftovers into the fillings for tacos, that's creativity. When we're stuck in a pattern of negative thinking and come up with a positive reframing of it, that's creativity, too.

My songwriting creativity feels different from my leftover-repurposing creativity. But they are related. I'm all for setting aside time to see the world poetically and pulling out my guitar to find the right chords, but in my life, even before I dedicated time to songwriting, I was already creative.

Art making is a turning of practical creativity into more abstract creativity, following a path of poetic thinking, and taking that path seriously. There is no reason to avoid making art because we think we are not creative. Everyone is already creative.

AGE

I've been leading songwriting retreats for about ten years now. Many of our songwriters have retired or semiretired from their jobs. They have some freedom with their schedules. They'd promised themselves they'd find time to write songs, and the year they turned fifty, sixty, seventy, or eighty turned out to be that time. The muse was right there, ready to jump in.

And they were in the good company of other songwriters who had figured out that age is unrelated to the strength of the creative force within us. Getting older is a gift to songwriters. Our minds get more complicated, our sense of interrelatedness grows, and our wisdom becomes deeper and more nuanced. On the one hand, the sense that everything is connected can make straightforward narratives more challenging, but, on the other, when we commit to our narratives, we also have so many more interesting things to say, we have the authority of true experience with which to say it, and we possess the knowledge that highly critical voices are often wrong.

DOING "WHAT IT TAKES" TO WRITE A SONG

I've heard it's important to "write every day." I disagree with two parts of that sentence: "write" and "every day." If inspiration comes at us, say, like a baseball, we want to break in a catcher's mitt to fit our hand, not contort our hand to fit a one-size glove. Writing every day doesn't fit every person.

Prescriptions can be superstitions. We love to counsel each other on how to write a great song if we "do what it takes." A great song is simply something that matters to us and, hopefully, an audience. And as for doing what it takes, we'd just be exhausted if we followed all the practices that others have prescribed. Apparently, a yoga practice, a specific amount of caffeine, very expensive wine, a relationship with God, a cigarette dangling out the side of my mouth while I'm typing on a typewriter, writing for two hours every morning, and an office space outside of my house will help me create "a great song." Or I can spin three times, spit to my left, and kiss my special pen.

My fellow retreat leader Raquel Vidal feels a song building up over a number of days. She wears many hats in her life, and each hat seems to bring her another insight or idea for that song. She says there's a time when all those song ideas get so big, she has to sit down with her instrument, give the song her full attention, get it all down in writing, and see what's there.

For some people, doing something every day is crucial to doing anything at all. They point out that in doing something every day, as with meditation or psychoanalysis, we often learn the most important things on the days we feel the least inspired to show up. "Every day" can be valuable.

I tried on the catcher's mitt of writing every day. I threw out most of what I wrote. Five years later, I showed up every day because I had a critical mass of ideas that required some sit-down shaping time. I knew that my fear of the unknown had kept me from spending time with my songs, and so I showed up every day for a few months (maybe not every day) to face my fears and to focus. That was the right call.

How I write is between me and me. How you come to write is between you and you. To make distinctions between correct and incorrect practices is to dance dangerously close to designating who is and is not a real writer.

In hopes of helping you widen the terrain of your creativity and confidence, I have an empathetic desire to help you go from inspiration to finished song, but to do it in a way, and on a timetable, that works for you.

THE POT ON THE WHEEL

Making a pot on a potter's wheel, or throwing it, as it's called, means putting a lump of clay in the middle of a round disc, called a wheel, and then, as the wheel quickly spins, centering the clay before delving into its middle to create a bowl or a vase.

To center the clay, the heel of one hand firmly, but gently, guides the clay up, while the side of the other hand, with equal force, pushes the clay down. The hands repeat this simultaneous scaling-up and pushing-down process until the clay is centered. Centering is crucial. When the clay is off-balance, the pot will collapse, or the clay will fly off the wheel.

Writing a song can be like centering clay on the wheel. One hand urges the song up with encouragement and a sense of lyrical and musical possibilities. The other hand keeps the song from teetering off balance. Paying attention to the Voice of the song is like the hand on top that guides the song to its own central core, confirming that twenty verses are just too much, even for a sea shanty, or that the word "ominous" carries the wrong weight in a song about a cat.

There are outside forces that influence the songwriter's centering hands on a potter's wheel. Sometimes they are the societal voices that play out in our heads. In modern pop culture, the hands are mismatched. The hand that values the commercial success of a finished product is strong and meaty, while the encouraging, upward-moving hand that values the open-ended creative process feels more weak and untrustworthy.

Ideally, we find places where the hands are matched. Teachers will help us find elegant rhymes but assure us that our clunky ones are no reason to stop writing. Friends will cheer for us at open mics and yell at the drunk guy at the bar who tells us to get off the stage. Family members will find a positive word for the sense we are making in our songs, even as they confess there are parts that they can't make out or understand. Schools will give us space to improve. Our cultural heroes will assure us that the risks they took were part of a path to their success.

It's important that both hands are working together in service of the song itself. We must find a way to encourage ourselves to explore, even as we value the discernment of what is and isn't working.

It's equally important to recognize whose constructive criticism is actually helpful. While I was telling some songwriters about one hand pushing up and one pushing down, I thought of some of the "hard" advice I had taken as tough love to keep me from writing drivel. Had I ever written a better song thanks to feedback that was disdainful and supercilious? I suddenly realized that feedback given with condescending and contemptuous attitudes had *never* been helpful to me or my songs—not once. It was only when feedback was given from the passenger seat, supportive of the song and unconditionally respectful of the songwriter, that the analogous shaping of feedback helped the song find its center.

OUR PROCESS IS THE *WHOLE* THING

"Garbage in, garbage out." Hmm.

I believe the expression "garbage in, garbage out" means that if we listen to Thelonious Monk, eat kale, and read T. S. Eliot, we'll put out "better" songs. On the flip side, if we listen to pop music, eat grocery-store pastries, and read cliché-ridden romances, we'll write "worse" songs. If I go by this measure, I will assume my songs are pretty bad.

I won't be coy. I know what it's like to hear something that I call "Brilliant! Brilliant!" that shines a beam of clarity into my soul, informs my life experience, and finds me saying, "I know my art will be better for having taken this in." We recognize the poetic precision, the emotional resonance, and the timeless truth in lines like Leonard Cohen's "There is a crack in everything. That's how the light gets in" and feel transported to a wiser place, often without even knowing why we feel so elevated. The actor Alan Arkin once said that the best art is the kind you can't even discuss as you're leaving the theater.

So, I could argue that reading a critically acclaimed, college syllabus–approved list of great books is the essential ingredient for creating great and acclaimed opuses to come. Certainly, there is a literary canon that has a great track record for jolting us into creating our most sophisticated works.

But *no*, the danger of assigning "necessary" and "great" books is too great. Perhaps John Prine would have downed a bottle of Jack Daniels and tripped into a rabbit hole of self-condemnation if he had thought the prerequisite of greatness was reading *The Iliad*. Perhaps Bill T. Jones would have danced only in his living room if he'd believed that George Balanchine's ballet was the only standard of quality choreography.

I've met every kind of artist in my touring life and seen that their whole selves, the whole refined and gaudy spectrum of colors they've take in, their whole extraordinary and ordinary day, their whole nutritious and highly processed food intake, and their whole complicated personalities have shown up to create a work of art.

They really don't have time to decide if they are pure enough to get to work on their songs. They just get to work. Lo and behold, the result is not tacky, banal, treacly, neurotic garbage. It's actually quite good. Whatever "goes in" and "comes out" in the writing of songs transcends the "garbage in, garbage out" analogy.

I used to think that what I "consumed" automatically exempted me from making meaningful art. I bought into the shame that there were some things we took into our minds and bodies that made us, top to bottom, trashy. I thought I shouldn't continue to write songs or go to open mics or share my songs, considering how many whoopie pies and soap operas I'd put into my system. But I plugged along, despite the risk that my work would be deemed "garbage." I wrote what I considered to be poetically honest. There was an audience for my songs, but even with that success, I assumed I'd created these things *despite* my garbage intake.

When I realized that my whole life, and the whole truth, informed my sensibility, not just the so-called good culture, good habits, and good food, I made art that was more intuitive, more generous of spirit, more artistically courageous, and, well, what I would call better. The only garbage was the shame itself.

WHAT DID YOU BRING BACK FOR ME?

It's so rewarding to explore the writing of a song, from inspiration to finishing touches, that I sometimes feel tempted to leave out what the audience gets out of hearing it. Rather than try to identify "good" songs over the years, I tried to distinguish what was communicated effectively in a song.

For five years or so, I told members of our songwriting retreats that I thought what the audience got out of a song came down to the single question of "What did you bring back for me?" How did the song hold something up at a new angle, crystallize a certain point, say something really funny, or provide some helpful wisdom?

But then I decided there are two answers to what we songwriters can bring back for the audience: One is the wisdom we impart. The other is the witness itself.

I saw how listeners could be moved by images and scenes that were beautifully or well observed without requiring a discernible nugget of wisdom. So, I added another thing that I noticed audiences were listening for: "Did you really go there?"

We can go to a place and bring back something that's more musical than lyrical. The wisdom and witness we bring can come in all forms. In the documentary *No Direction Home*, Bobby Neuwirth says that in the Greenwich Village of the early '60s, when a person came back from a concert, friends would ask, "Did they have something to say?" Neuwirth said "something to say" could mean a lot of things. A jazz performance, a fiddle tune, and a dance performance can "really go there," "bring something back for us," or accomplish both things.

We are the first audience members of our own songs, and we can ask ourselves whether we really went to a place, found something to bring back, and had something to say. Depending on our relationship with our creativity, the inner audience member might come back with a lot of self-invalidating criticisms in answer to those questions.

So, we can start by checking in with ourselves, but let's not stop with ourselves! Let's find some people we can trust, or a friendly open mic, or, if you're like me, try it out on an audience or two. I played the first lines of "February" at a small concert in Hartford, Connecticut (thanks for the encouragement, Ed McKeon!), and the first verse of "As Cool as I Am" at the Kuumbwa Jazz Center in Santa Cruz (the all-women audience gave me a thumbs-up!).

When we as songwriters have written more than three or four songs, we are rarely just writing for ourselves as the audience. We get curious about who will receive our message in a bottle and about what will connect. I don't want to be too reductive with the criteria of "Did you really go there?" and "What did you bring back for us?" for what makes a song "good." But I have seen, time and again, how audiences respond to songs that bring them something that feels both new and true.

THE OTHER SONG

You didn't write the song by the well-known and beloved songwriter of your youth, *the* song that was so important to you that you thought you shouldn't even bother to write a song yourself.

But then, you did write a song. You took the time and care; you heard the Voice and followed the Voice. You took that chance to let the song become itself.

Someday, someone might walk up to you and say that your song really did something for them in their lives, that it was valuable to them. It's not the song that you heard in your youth that was so important to you.

And you know why? Because you wrote the other song. It is not the song that another person wrote. It's the song only you could write. And there was a person who needed that other song. You wrote the other song.

WHY WE SHOULD ALL GO OUT AND WRITE A SONG THAT MATTERS

When I go to a concert, two things are happening. I am taking in the lyrics and music. I am also taking in the collective experience that we are all having, the performer, stage crew, house manager, promoter, and audience. We are all participating in an event with the express purpose of experiencing our lives poetically.

Art in general reminds me that there are things we call meaningful. Time is an impersonal force, and life itself can feel airy and insubstantial, but when I hear a song that I love, something catches and holds me the way gravity holds us to the ground. There is resonance; there is traction.

When we take the time to write a song, we get an even deeper understanding of what songs can do. Not only do we value a poetic reality that gives meaning to our lives, but we are also able to better appreciate the contribution that others have made by offering their own poetic perspectives in songs.

We're often told that artists are narcissists, because there's some pop-culture message that putting art into the world is a call for attention and adoration. Try writing a song and playing it for someone. Do we want to know if we're "great," or do we want to know if we have something to contribute? Searching for self-worth through the creation of art is hoping that something is of worth, has something to say, and has traction in the fast-moving airiness of time. The songwriter is bringing something new into the world, and even if it's light or sappy or silly, they'll want to know if they reached you, if they helped you, if they moved you, and if they participated in making your life feel more meaningful in a way that art has done for them.

I believe that writing songs is good for humanity, so off I go, courting inspiration and taking it very seriously. I'm walking down the street and I hear a six-note progression with the words "under a dog-moon sky," I look up the names of the moons (Hunter moon in October, Harvest moon in September, and so on), and decide to create my own Dog-moon month. I listen for the ambiance underneath the melody, catch the rhythm and feel, make it pretty, think about how it might connect with my life, see what rhymes, notice the Voice emerging, go to that place, ask myself what really happened, check in with whether I'm really saying what I want to say, find the little twists and turns that keep my song beautiful and interesting, work through and finesse my phrasing, make sure all of my little details feel right to me, and come to the world with a finished song. Hopefully, it brings something new and true to its listeners.

I'm doing it for me, I'm doing it for the world, and I'm doing it because in my experience, sharing what matters to me helps others remember what is important to them. I'm trusting that my poetic reality gives ordinary reality more traction.

The only real narcissism that I've found is cynicism. Cynics demand that we stick with a static worldview where nothing's worth doing. They don't entertain diverse poetic realities. They like to control things instead of create things. Cynics don't write songs. They sit on their porches and throw crushed beer cans at people who write songs.

But if that cynic stops, looks down at the squashed can he's about to throw, and thinks it looks like a space capsule, maybe a little phrase will emerge about a space capsule landing in a small town. Maybe it lands in a harbor or a fishing pond, and maybe that space-capsule idea will have a sort of ambiance that sounds like a really cool early-seventies rock song, and maybe Neil Armstrong will come out of the capsule and someone's mom will row out and bring him home for dinner, and she'll serve the fish that her kids caught in the pond, and everyone will agree that Neil is the biggest fish they've ever caught.

And that cynic will go inside and find an old guitar and start to play some chords and write down the words about his family and Neil Armstrong in the fishing pond, and he won't feel cynical about it. It won't feel like a self-indulgent thing he's doing; it will feel a little challenging and strangely worthwhile, and a month later, he'll be at an open mic and he'll get up on the stage, which feels not at all narcissistic and actually pretty terrifying, and he will perform this song, because this song matters to him and . . . who knows?

ACKNOWLEDGMENTS

Tom Todoroff is the artistic director of a New York City acting conservatory that he created with his wife and partner, Emily Moulton Todoroff. When Tom saw how much I loved teaching a college course, he told me I had to lead a songwriting retreat.

I said, "I can't do that. I can't teach anyone how to get a record contract or put together a press pack. If I were going to lead a songwriting retreat, it would have to be for people who really, actually, want to write songs. It would have to be called something like 'Writing a Song that Matters.'"

Tom said, "So why don't you call it 'Writing a Song that Matters'?"

I'm forever grateful to Tom and Emily for recognizing that this retreat would be as meaningful to me as writing and performing my own songs.

I am also very thankful for my colleagues Raquel Vidal, Michele Gedney, Rick Gedney (who also helped write the music chapters), KJ Denhert, Lara Demberg Voloto, Amanda Gates-Elston, and Kellie Lin Knott.

Garrison Institute and Omega Institute both provided beautiful homes for our retreat. It was an honor to be there.

I don't know how to begin to thank the people who have attended the retreat over the years. They, and our guest artists, cocreated a musical world of trust, fun, and mutual support. Every retreat was greater than the sum of its already magical parts.

Thanks also to Patty Romanoff, Toby Shimin, Bryn Roberts, Nerissa and Katryna Nields, Lisa Arzt, Michael, Taya, and Stephen Robinson, Jamie Raskin and Sarah Bloom, the Williams family, Lucy Wainwright Roche, Ben Schafer, Anthony Arnove, Kathleen Denney, Seth Rappaport, Patty Smythe, Beth Gershuny, Kirsti Reeve, Kate Bennis, Anne Weiss, Maggie Siff and Lucy Ratliff (love you gals), Bergin O'Malley, Julie Wolf, Cliff Eberhardt, Jim Infantino, John Dear, Lucy Kaplansky, Richard Shindell, Charlie Hunter, Ward Williams, and all the generous, good people I worked with who believed in the things that mattered to me.